every
step
a prayer

every
step
a prayer

WALKING AS SPIRITUAL PRACTICE

thomas r. hawkins

UPPER
ROOM BOOKS®
NASHVILLE

Cover: LUCAS Art & Design, Jenison, MI
Cover art: Masterful Images
Interior design: Perfect Type, Nashville, Tennessee

LIBRARY OF CONGRESS CATALOGING-IN-PUBLICATION DATA
Hawkins, Thomas R.
    Every step a prayer : walking as spiritual practice / Thomas R. Hawkins.
        pages cm
    Includes bibliographical references.
    ISBN 978-0-8358-1521-5 (print)—ISBN 978-0-8358-1532-1 (mobi)—ISBN 978-0-8358-1522-2 (epub)
    1. Prayer—Christianity. 2. Walking—Religious aspects—Christianity. I. Title.
    BV215.H39 2016
    248—dc23
                                                                    2015032575

To

ROBERT AND JONATHAN

Walking Companions and Fellow Pilgrims

Buen Camino

CONTENTS

EVERY STEP A PRAYER

Everyone was in a good mood at the August church council meeting. Jenni reported on the successful Fourth of July walkathon that had raised funds for Habitat for Humanity. Mike announced that he would coordinate the annual CROP Walk for Hunger. Betsy expressed excitement about the church's participation in the American Cancer Society's Relay for Life. The church's team had already exceeded the fund-raising goal.

LaToya commented that she and her friends go to a shopping mall and walk its hallways. Luis remarked that he too had been walking. He had marched at the state capitol to protest cuts in the social services budget. Claude added that his son and daughter-in-law were doing a lot more walking. Clogged expressways and bumper-to-bumper traffic had left them too exhausted to enjoy their suburban home. So they had sold it and moved back into the city. Now they walk to work and to go shopping.

Joy jokingly suggested that our church council might like to adopt her boss's latest approach for staff meetings. Since walking increases people's creativity, they now walk around the building for Monday staff meetings.

As I listened to everyone's comments, I began to think of all the people in my congregation who were taking to their feet. Marta has a new dog and gets up to walk her puppy. Kate and Jack recently joined our congregation because their home is within walking distance of the church. Committed environmentalists, they walk as much as possible to reduce their carbon footprint. Each summer Candace walks sections of the Appalachian Trail with her friends. Several members drive to a wellness center, have their vital signs checked, and walk a treadmill under a nurse's supervision. Max coordinates a senior high adventure camp that features hiking in Colorado during July.

Despite our North American romance with automobiles, walking is making a comeback. Six in ten Americans report that they walked for fun, transportation, or exercise. More than 145 million Americans say they walk for health. In the last five years, the number of people who walk for exercise has increased by 6 percent.

Walking also plays a role in funding many national and local charities. American charities and congregations annually sponsor almost 40,000 fund-raising walk/run/rideathons that attract millions of participants. In recent years the top thirty such events raised a total of $1.6 billion. Members of my congregation walk or run in charity fund-raisers every year.

Americans also walk in protests, parades, or marches that seek to shape public opinion, influence the political process, or celebrate their heritage or identity. The National Park Service annually issues approximately 3,800 permits for marches on Washington DC's National Mall.

I am an avid walker. Walking trails lace the woods surrounding my family's home, and every morning and evening I walk our family dog, Spenser, along them. On vacation, my favorite activity comes in walking through urban and rural landscapes, taking in the sights, sounds, and smells. Some of my favorite childhood memories include walks with my grandfather to hunt for mushrooms or to dig sassafras roots for tea.

Until that August church council meeting, however, I had never considered all the opportunities for walking that our congregation's ministries build in. Nor had I realized the extent to which members integrated walking into their daily routines.

Beneath our society's renewed interest in walking lies a yearning to slow down in a 24/7 world; to reconnect to the natural world in a crowded, technological society; and to express our protest in a political climate where many people feel they have a vote but not a voice. This deep yearning intersects with the spiritual resources of our Christian faith, which has always understood walking as a means to and an expression of prayer. As we rediscover how every step can be a prayer, we walk a well-marked path traveled by our Christian forebears who understood that walking—like many other simple, everyday gestures—can be a spiritual discipline and an act of prayer.

The following chapters invite us to explore walking as a discipline that can inform our spiritual life. They examine how taking to our feet in worship reminds us that walking is a Christian spiritual practice that can deepen our awareness of God's Spirit in our lives. They discuss the anatomy and physiology of walking and how the movement of our feet influences the movement of our mind, our hearts, and our breathing, all of which shape our receptivity to God's Spirit in us and our world.

We seldom walk alone. Even when we are solitary walkers, we walk roads and paths that others have traveled before us and that still hold the memory and imprint of their presence. In the same way, we as Christians are never alone but are always surrounded by a great cloud of witnesses, the communion of saints, who support us as we run the race set before us in our own lifetimes.

Finally, our feet typically lead us both across our doorsteps into the world and then guide us back home. In the same way, walking as a spiritual practice directs us to our ultimate homecoming in God's love and grace.

The book of Genesis tells us that from the very beginning, God wanted us as faithful walking partners. (See Genesis 3:8.) The Bible's poets and prophets continually invite us to return to the God who requires that we do justice, love mercy, and walk humbly alongside our divine companion. (Read Micah 6:8.) By entering into these pages we respond to the invitation to discover how walking as a spiritual practice can lead us along the paths of righteousness, guide us to still waters, and restore our souls. (See Psalm 23.)

At the end of each chapter you will find questions and activities for further reflection. Each chapter includes a specific exercise or exercises designed to help you walk prayerfully. I typically walk on a sidewalk or in a natural area. In times of inclement weather, I walk on a treadmill. You may adapt these exercises to whatever setting is available and comfortable to you.

You may use these activities and questions to guide your personal reflection. If you are reading this book with others, discuss the questions and your experience of the activities together when you meet. As the basis for a small-group experience, you will want to include a feedback or debriefing time that allows everyone to share their responses to the suggested walking activity.

I encourage you to create a special "walking journal" to keep track of your observations, questions, and insights. Use your journal to record what days you walked, where you walked, how long you walked, and how far you walked. If you have set walking goals, these records can help you measure your progress. One worthwhile goal would be to work toward walking ten thousand steps daily. Start where you are, and add more steps each day.

 **one**

Teach Me Your Paths

Most walking paths are well marked: a yellow dot painted on a tree, a small arrow telling us which way to turn, or three blue stripes painted onto a post set into the ground. But sometimes the cues are more difficult to discern: a slightly rutted track in the ground where people's shoes have compressed the soil or a subtle change in the landscape where the passing of many boots has stunted the grass. Because not all trails are well marked, walkers can take an occasional wrong turn. Encountering less clear pathways gives me a new appreciation for Psalm 107:4-5, which reads as follows: "Some wandered in desert wastes, finding no way to an inhabited town; hungry and thirsty, their soul fainted within them."

My guidebook once told me to follow the mowed path through a field until I reached a stone fence with a gate. Unfortunately, I was walking in mid-August and thousands of sheep had grazed the field for most of the summer. I found it impossible to tell where a mowing machine might have mechanically cut the grass and where thousands of small teeth had cropped it close to the ground. I consequently ended up hungry and thirsty at the wrong end of a very large pasture. The sun was setting and the nearest inn was miles away. Lost on an empty moor in northern England, I felt my soul fainting within me.

Another time, I followed what seemed to be the main trail. The rutted ground and worn grass suggested that I should keep following this path. I continued for more than an hour before I discovered that it was only an animal trackway that I could no longer follow because it dropped into a steep ravine full of brambles. Human feet had not worn this path. Hundreds of deer hooves had created it.

To avoid getting lost, I always look for clues that other walkers have left behind them. These signs tell me that I am on the right path. In the same way, other Christian believers have marked out particular practices as cues that help me find my way to God. They point me toward well-traveled pathways where I can cultivate a deeper love, knowledge, and service of God and neighbor.

Scientists have a name for this phenomenon. They call it stigmergy. Stigmergy is a form of self-organization and indirect coordination where one person or animal leaves a trace in the environment that stimulates others to repeat the same action. Actions build indirectly on one another over time to produce a visible structure or pattern. This emergent pattern then directs others to behave in the same fashion. A sheep wanders across a pasture, following the tender stalks of grass. The lone sheep presses down the grass, eats off the stems, and leaves the smell of its urine in the soil as it goes along. These subtle markers become cues that guide other sheep to follow the same path. As more and more sheep follow these signs and cues, they crush the grass still more. They leave behind still stronger traces of their scent. Gradually, the path becomes clearer and clearer. At some point, all the sheep can identify this broad, wide path that rambles across the pasture.

Stigmergy provides the answer to my father's perennial complaint about roads with endless bends and curves: "Who designed this road?" he would mutter. "It must have been built by engineers who were following a cow path." In fact, it probably *did* follow an animal trackway that later became a human footpath, which engineers made into a highway sometime in the last century. As stigmergy would predict, people kept following the same cues and signals as the road widened from an animal trackway to a highway. Stigmergy allows complex, coordinated action without any immediate presence or explicit communication. This underappreciated concept explains how systems organize from the bottom up.

Stigmergy explains how Christian spiritual practices like walking actually work. In these practices, simple, everyday human gestures become signposts that direct us from one way of being in the world to another. In worship, we rehearse these gestures. We distill and intensify them so that a clear pattern of cues and signals shape our lives, moving us from one way of being human toward another. As more people engage in these practices, the path becomes clearer and more focused. No one has to talk about what we should or should not do. Everyone simply follows the signs and cues that others have left behind them. It is a bottom-up way of organizing the Christian life. Stigmergic practices quietly direct people toward a certain way of life.

In Hebrews 12, the author reminds us that we are surrounded by a great cloud of witnesses who invite us to lay aside every weight and sin that cling so closely and "run with perseverance the race that is set before us, looking to Jesus the pioneer and perfecter of our faith" (vv. 1-2). Having rehearsed in Hebrews 11 the stigmergic signals of faithfulness to God that patriarchs, matriarchs, prophets, and monarchs across the ages have laid down, the author admonishes readers to "lift your drooping hands and strengthen your weak knees, and make straight paths for your feet" (vv. 12-13).

Every Step a Prayer

Christian practices that incorporate everyday gestures and actions typically involve our bodies: We speak, sing, eat, wash, or bow. We walk. By investing these gestures with new meanings, Christian practices shift our way of being in the world. The Incarnation means that God invites us to experience our physical, embodied existence as a dwelling place of the holy. As Paul says, "I appeal to you therefore, brothers and sisters, by the mercies of God, to present your bodies as a living sacrifice, holy and acceptable to God, which is your spiritual worship" (Rom. 12:1).

Therefore, all physical gestures are charged with spiritual possibilities, and all spiritual practices can employ physical gestures legitimately. By acknowledging concrete, down-to-earth activities—eating, drinking, making decisions, generous sharing, hospitality, and walking—as the means through which God comes to us and by which we participate in God's work in the world, Christian practices remind us of the sensible, everyday qualities of Christian life. Christian faith involves more than simply believing certain things about God. It is also a matter of practicing our faith. "Be doers of the word, and not merely hearers. . . . Those who look into the perfect law, the law of liberty, and persevere, being not hearers who forget but doers who act—they will be blessed in their doing" (James 1:22, 25).

Practices can establish a deep, embodied connection between us and God, whose grace permeates all things. They join us with each other, with Jesus, and with the communion of saints throughout time and space in an embodied way of life that overflows with God's love for us and all creation. Practices awaken in us the same love and devotion that Jesus' first disciples must have felt in his presence.

Christian practices are thought-full. They invite us to a reflective, thoughtful way of life. They guide us toward increased mindfulness of how we live a life that becomes the gospel. Christian practices enable us to experience everyday gestures and actions as channels of grace through which we glimpse the depths of God's love and care.

These practices are not burdensome tasks or rules required to become "good Christians." Instead, they are gifts from God that nurture openness and receptivity to divine love that streams continuously through the people, events, and places of our world. Walking represents one such Christian practice.

Walking is not only a way to move ourselves from one place to another but also a Christian practice imbued with the same intent as every other Christian practice: to guide us into a way of being human that bears witness to God's work of healing a broken, wounded creation.

When I walk, my life slows down. Rather than speed past the world around me, sealed in my car with the radio playing, I move slowly. Moving at the speed of my feet, I hear the sounds of birds, insects, and the wind blowing through the trees. The rhythm of my footfalls invites me into an awareness of myself and the world around me. This awareness leads me beyond creation to the Creator. When a friend and I walk across the campus where I teach, our conversation takes on a different quality than when we sit in an office or around a lunchroom table. Walking, like all Christian practices, makes me more open and receptive, more mindful and aware.

Walking is woven into many parts of Christian worship, hinting at how it functions as a Christian practice. In the church I serve, acolytes walk down the aisle to light candles as worship begins. They return at the close of the service to walk the light of Christ out into the world. The choir and pastors walk down the center aisle in a procession as the congregation sings the opening hymn. People leave their pews and walk around the sanctuary to share the peace of Christ. Worship leaders walk into the midst of the congregation to read the Gospel lesson. Ushers walk up and down the aisles to gather worshipers' tithes. They walk the offering plates forward as we sing the Doxology.

When my church celebrates the Eucharist, worshipers walk forward to receive the bread and cup. Patrick, a member of the congregation, now uses a cane as a result of a stroke. He moves very slowly as he comes forward to receive Communion. Patrick could sit in the pew and let the servers bring the bread and cup to him, but coming down the aisle expresses his gratitude to God for walking beside him during his hospitalization and recovery. "Every step I take is a prayer. It's how I praise God for my recovery," he says. Everybody waits patiently behind Patrick as he walks forward because they all know what it means to him.

On the third Sunday of each month the church takes up a special offering for hunger relief at the beginning of worship. People walk forward to drop pennies, dimes, and quarters into a large metal bowl, making it ring with the sound of offerings. Coming forward with coins enacts in a concrete, visible way the congregation's commitment to feeding the physically and spiritually hungry. Church members can feel the energy in the room as people come down the aisles. Walking reminds us that we are a pilgrim people on a journey toward God's future, seeking to be signs of healing in a broken world. Passing the offering plates in the pews would not have the same impact. It might be quieter, less confusing, and more efficient, but symbolism and spiritual power would be lost.

During Lent and Easter, my congregants take to their feet more frequently in worship. On Ash Wednesday, they walk forward to have the sign of the cross made on their foreheads. They gather for Lenten midweek services of evening prayer, which begin when someone walks down the aisle with a lit candle and places it on a stand. On Palm Sunday they walk in a procession that begins in the fellowship hall and concludes in the sanctuary. On Good Friday, they walk the Stations of the Cross to accompany Jesus on his way of sorrow and suffering. At the Easter Vigil on the Saturday night before Easter, church members gather in a garden courtyard outside the church. Following prayers and songs, they walk in a procession to the sanctuary for the first celebration of the Resurrection. Throughout Lent, we receive invitations to walk with Jesus as he journeys to Jerusalem for his passion, death, and resurrection. These opportunities for walking throughout Lent offer a clue to its critical importance in the Christian life.

"Whoever sings, prays twice," a choir director noted. But no one has ever said to me, "Whoever walks, prays twice." A spiritual director once asked me to calculate the percentage of worship that involves spoken or silent prayers: opening prayers, prayers for illumination before the reading of scripture, prayers of confession, prayers over the offering, or pastoral prayers. She emphasized the centrality of prayer in worship and the need for worship leaders to be people of prayer if they are to lead the Christian assembly in praise and prayer. But no spiritual director has ever asked me to list all the times when people walk in worship.

We take our many ways of walking during worship for granted without pausing to consider their spiritual significance or their connection to other times and places that we take to our feet. When we think about walking in worship, we usually see it only as a practical matter. But walking in worship is so much more than a practical matter.

Worship as Rehearsal Time

In Christian worship, we use the familiar gestures of everyday life to proclaim God's activity in our lives. In worship, we rehearse in a distilled, concentrated way the gestures—the practices—through which we grow in the love, knowledge, and service of God. We stand when we recite the creed, for example, as a rehearsal for all the occasions when we will stand up for our beliefs and values in our workplaces, homes, and neighborhoods. We share our tithes and offerings in worship to practice living generously with others.

The times that we take to our feet in worship are not merely incidental, random movements. When we take to our feet in weekly worship, we rehearse the dance steps with which we move to the music of God's grace throughout the week. Recognition of how walking is woven into the fabric of Christian worship acknowledges it as a Christian practice in which every step is a prayer. When we take to our feet in worship, we rehearse together how God desires us to live as God's pilgrim people in the world.

Just as athletes and musicians need regular opportunities to rehearse their skills and hone their techniques, we need rehearsal time for Christian practices. Worship etches into our habits and muscles the movements of mind and spirit that enable us to participate in God's project of redeeming a broken world. Walking in worship prepares us for walking to alleviate hunger or to oppose violence against women. It gives us cues for how to walk the corridors of power where people make decisions that affect the lives of many.

Without such opportunities, we can wander off the path and find ourselves in some cul-de-sac of existence. Our frantic schedules can throw us off balance. Cable news and social media distract us with an endless tsunami of information and images that encourage us to skim along the surface of life. Living in the shallows of being, we never "taste and see that the LORD is good" (Ps. 34:8). Speed limits our ability to live mindfully in God's moment-by-moment care. Christian practices such as walking, eating, or washing help us stay on the path that leads to a life of fullness and spiritual depth.

When we take to our feet in worship, we are being invited to place before God all those men and women with whom and for whom we walk during the week: the elderly parents whose arms we hold as they walk from the bedroom to the kitchen or the child whose hand we take as we walk across a busy street. Our walking in worship reminds us of our daily call to solidarity with the refugee who has walked to safety across a desolate war zone. It becomes an act of confession and penitence for all the people we have walked away from because we were too afraid, too busy, or too self-absorbed to care about them. The places, people, and purposes for which we walk are gathered together, sanctified, forgiven, and blessed as we take to our feet in worship. When we walk as a Christian practice, we silently pray with the psalmist, "Make me to know your ways, O Lord; teach me your paths" (25:4).

Walking in worship forms us into a people who are moving steadily toward the New Jerusalem, where God will dwell with God's people; death will be no more, and God will wipe away every tear. When we begin to rehearse music, the director usually says "take it from the top." But when it comes to a spiritual practice like walking, it would be more accurate to say, "Take it from the bottom" because the spiritual practice of walking begins with the soles of our feet.

Walking Suggestions

Each chapter will conclude with some suggestions for prayerful walks. You may wish to try one or more of these suggestions as an activity during the week. If you are reading this book as a group, you may choose to try these suggestions together.

Each chapter will also conclude with some questions for further reflection, which invite you to consider specific connections between what you have read and your personal experience. If you are reading this book as a group, the questions can serve as a basis for group discussion. As we start our journey, here are two simple suggestions to help us begin.

Keep a Written Log of Your Walking

You may wish to purchase a notebook or journal in which you keep a written log of where and when you walk over the course of a day or a week. If you have a pedometer, keep track of how many steps or miles you walk each day (you can purchase an inexpensive pedometer at most sporting goods stores). Then ask yourself the following questions:

- How much time do I spend walking?
- Where do I walk?
- With whom do I predictably walk?
- What times of day do I typically walk?
- What motivates me to walk? leisure and relaxation? spending time with friends? my health?
- What does my pattern of walking say about my life?

Make some notes in a journal about what you discover, and share your observations with others in a small group or spiritual friendship.

Go for a Walk

Go for a walk sometime this week. Just walk. Do not plan your walk for a purpose, such as going to a store, visiting a friend, or taking your dog outside. Just walk. Let your feet take you where they want to go. Leave your iPod and smartphone behind. Be alone with your feet and your thoughts. When you return, make notes about the experience of walking:

- What did you observe in the world around you as you walked? How does the world look different when you walk instead of drive?
- What thoughts came to you while walking? Did you notice anything different about the kind of thoughts that arose?

- What did you find difficult about this exercise? What was easy?
- What did you notice about your body as you walked?
- What did you observe about the interplay between the physical motion of walking and your emotions?

Questions for Further Reflection

1. Using your church bulletin, examine all the moments when people take to their feet in worship. Who is walking at different times during the service (worship leaders, congregants, choir, acolytes, ushers, readers)? What are they or others doing when they take to their feet? What symbolism could these moments hold? What do they model about how to live as a disciple of Jesus?

2. When have you walked in or helped with a charity fundraiser? What motivated your participation? What could you learn from this experience that would inform the Christian practice of walking in worship and in life?

3. When did you last walk in a parade or march? What was this experience like for you? What can you learn from this experience about the Christian spiritual practice of walking?

4. What are some current practices or Christian disciplines that you have incorporated into your spiritual life? In what ways do these shape how you live? believe? practice your faith?

5. Describe a time when you got lost. What did you feel
    when you realized you were lost? What strengths or
    resources did you call upon to find your way?

 two

Prime Mover

It is a moment every parent anticipates. When toddlers take their first steps, parents exhibit understandable excitement. The excitement fades quickly, however. Those first steps soon cease to be childhood's supreme achievement. They instead become just another memory tucked away in a baby book. Once they discover their feet, toddlers are immediately given wheels: tricycles, Big Wheels, and Cozy Coupes.

Parents have many reasons to be excited when toddlers learn to walk. Walking upright, a uniquely human achievement, distinguishes us from almost every other mammal. Kangaroos are also bipeds; but they do not walk. They hop. Birds walk or run on two legs, but they have tails to balance themselves. The nearest species, the great apes, can briefly waddle along on two feet, but it is not their preferred or most efficient means of locomotion. Human beings, on the other hand, are true bipeds.

Fearfully and Wonderfully Made

Our physical frame is designed for walking upright on two feet. We are not made for standing or sitting. Our spine is not straight but jointed and doubly curved. Its shape propels us forward. Our hips are also part of our design for walking on two feet. Flexible ball-and-socket joints provide mobility and fluid movement of hips and legs. With each stride, our legs swing freely in these sockets so that as we walk our weight shifts smoothly from one side of the body to the other. The primary function of more than half our muscles is to help us walk. The muscles in our feet, legs, hips, and backs contract and release with every step we take. Striding forward, we throw our arms and shoulders back and forth to balance our bodies.

Walking also plays an important role in supporting our circulatory system. Our arteries have muscles that contract and release to pump blood throughout the body. Veins, on the other hand, lack similar muscles. Above the waist, veins rely on the pressure of arterial flow and gravity to move blood to the heart. Below the waist, they depend on the contraction and release of the muscles in our feet, calves, thighs, and abdomen—together with the diaphragm—to move blood to the heart. As we walk, our leg muscles literally "milk" the blood back to the heart. In a certain sense, walking serves as our "second heart."

We can trace many of our modern health problems to the sedentary lifestyle we impose on physical bodies made for walking. Studies have linked extended periods of sitting to increased likelihood of developing type 2 diabetes, obesity, and cardiovascular disease, all of which lead to an elevated risk of premature death. A friend of mine suggested that instead of delivering bad news with the expression, "Are you sitting down?" we should instead say, "Are you standing up?"

The psalmist exclaims, "I praise you, for I am fearfully and wonderfully made. Wonderful are your works; that I know very well. . . . How weighty to me are your thoughts, O God! How vast is the sum of them!" (139:14, 17). We are truly fearfully and wonderfully made to walk. Everything about the human body is made for walking. The effects of human locomotion do not stop with our physical makeup, however. They also extend to our mental and emotional capacities.

In the Beginning Was the Foot

Scientists increasingly believe that our ability to walk upright emerged before the human brain developed into its current shape and size. So walking has shaped human consciousness itself. The area of the brain most closely related to motor control is the cerebellum, located at the back of the brain and about the size of a small fist. While the cerebellum constitutes only one-tenth of the brain's volume, it contains nearly one half of the brain's neurons. The cerebellum manages neural communication about motor movement; it also has massive connections into all other regions of the brain, including those areas that influence thought, memory, attention, and spatial perception. Some forty million nerve fibers feed information back and forth between the cerebellum and the neocortex, our thinking brain.

Why is this significant? In the cerebellum motor movements and thought processes come together. Brief, quick thought processes precede all motor activity: setting goals, analyzing variables, predicting outcomes, and executing movement. Mental thought thus develops out of muscle movement. To pick up a water glass, I am setting a goal. To reach this goal, I have to analyze the distance between my hand and the glass and then decide how to move my hand. My eyes are continuously gathering information about these motor movements. Based on this feedback, I decide upon slight muscle adjustments that bring my hand precisely to my goal. All these mental and motor processes are happening along neural pathways that coalesce in the cerebellum. The neural pathways that coordinate and direct motor movements are the same neural pathways for thought processes such as predicting, sequencing, timing, or even rehearsing a task.

Thinking on Our Feet

It should therefore come as no surprise that a motor movement like walking, which relates intimately to everything from the circulation of our blood to the flexing of our muscles, would exert a powerful influence over the neural patterns that shape our mental processes. The pattern of our motor movements becomes the pattern of our thoughts. We might even say that the movement of our feet becomes the movement of our minds. Although John's Gospel (1:1) begins, "In the beginning was the Word," we might just as easily say, "In the beginning was the foot." Walking is how we move through space. Language is how we describe this experience.

This relationship between physical movement and the mind explains why we have such a rich and nuanced vocabulary to describe how we walk. We ramble, amble, stroll, or stride. We meander and mosey. We roam and rove. We parade or promenade or plod. We even pace and trudge. When overly confident, we swagger. Under difficult conditions, we stumble along and stagger.

We use descriptions of walking to represent people's emotions, outlooks on life, and personalities. We would never say that a shy person "swaggered" into the room or that a brave soldier "meandered" into battle. When we describe someone as "creepy," we are not just describing how he or she walks. To call people "sure-footed" is to convey something about their personalities and not just how they move physically. Our terminology of walking represents a reservoir of metaphors and analogies for human feelings and attitudes.

We pepper our language with expressions about our feet. A good leader walks the talk. A poor one puts his foot in his mouth. We invite people to take a load off their feet. Dissatisfied church members vote with their feet and drop out. I dance with two left feet. When my father drove, he had a lead foot. I always try to put my best foot forward. Occasionally I shoot myself in the foot. One of my friends usually lands on her feet regardless of her mistakes. Another acquaintance often gets off on the wrong foot with a new supervisor. Observations about our feet are not simply literal, physical descriptions of how we walk.

As human beings, we have a foot-focused vocabulary. This vocabulary serves as the framework through which we perceive our world and communicate with one another. We can even trace the modern English word for learning back to the experience of walking. Its Proto-Indo-European root is *leis*, which means "track" or "furrow." To learn is quite literally to "follow a track" or to "walk a path." We learn on the soles of our feet.

The Bible's Foot-Focused Vocabulary

If the movement of our feet shapes the movement of our thoughts and emotions, then it certainly affects our spiritual lives. If our physical bodies atrophy when deprived of physical movement, then just as surely our spirits atrophy when we cease to walk with God. Walking as a spiritual practice is more than a pleasant walk through the countryside or a way to stay physically fit. It influences how we interpret and experience God's presence in our lives and our world. Just as Christian worship encompasses many opportunities to take to our feet, Christian scripture frequently describes knowing or loving God in terms of walking a particular path or way.

Our foot-focused vocabulary has profoundly influenced the development of biblical poetry, prophecy, and prayer. As Psalm 25 prays, "To you, O LORD, I lift up my soul. O my God, in you I trust.... Make me to know your ways, O LORD; teach me your paths. Lead me in your truth, and teach me. . . . [The LORD] instructs sinners in the way . . . and teaches the humble his way. All the paths of the LORD are steadfast love and faithfulness" (vv. 1, 4–5, 8–10). In Genesis, God walks in the garden in the cool of the evening, looking for the companionship of the First Man and the First Woman. The children of Israel eat the Passover meal as they prepare to walk from slavery to freedom. They carry walking sticks in their hands and wear sandals on their feet.

Nestled within the book of Psalms we find a small collection of "songs of ascent" or pilgrim psalms. Psalms 120–134 represent a compilation of songs that pilgrims sang as they walked to Jerusalem for the celebration of the Temple festivals. These psalms reveal how walking became prayer for the children of Israel. "Happy is everyone who fears the LORD, who walks in his ways," chants Psalm 128:1. In the New Testament, Paul, who traveled mostly by foot on his missionary journeys, frequently describes Christian discipleship as a path that we walk. Believers are to walk by the Spirit (Gal. 5:16, NIV). We who are baptized walk in newness of life (Rom. 6:4). Disciples of Jesus are to walk by faith (2 Cor. 5:7).

The men and women of the Bible did not fly or ride. They walked. Their world was circumscribed by how far their feet could carry them. When I calculate how long a walk will take me, I usually estimate that I can walk about three miles per hour, which is the historical average. A day's journey on foot over rocky, unpaved roads in ancient Israel fell between sixteen and twenty-three miles per day. The English word *journey* derives from the French word *jour* or "day." A journey originally signified the distance a person could travel by foot in one *jour* or a single day.

The Bible's authors lived in a three-mile-per-hour world defined by feet rather than wheels or wings. Their world was much smaller, but they knew it more intimately. When I walk, I notice the squirrels in the trees and flattened grass where a rabbit has passed. I encounter smells, textures, and sounds that otherwise I would not notice. I sense more deeply my connection to the natural world around me. When I drive, I see only a blur of people and objects, fleeting and vanishing. Pieces of landscape flash before my eyes in swift succession. The faster I move, the less I experience. Speed deadens my senses.

A few years ago, my son Robert and I walked the Hadrian's Wall Trail in northern England. It took us five days to walk about eighty miles. Before we began at Newcastle-on-Tyne and headed east toward the Solway coast, we flew to England. Our air flight encompassed thirty-eight hundred miles and took seven hours. Five days to travel eighty miles. Seven hours to fly thirty-eight hundred miles. The chasm between these two trips involves more than time and distance; it involves *quality* of experience. When we flew to England, we saw only the inside of a metal tube rocketing through the air. Walking, we saw flowers and sheep, cattle and horses, ancient stone walls and Roman forts.

Walking as a Spiritual Practice

As modern women and men, we move from one interior space to another. We leave the interior of our homes and enter the interior of our cars. We step out of the car and go inside an office, mall, or shop. Clocks and convenience govern this seamless movement from one interior space to another. Consequently, we never really inhabit an "outside." Enclosed within cocoons of our own making, we easily make ourselves the center of our own private worlds. We never experience ourselves as part of a larger world that moves to creation's own rhythms. We lose touch not just with creation but with its Creator.

Walking slows our pace. The spiritual practice of walking reminds us we live from God who is the center of all things rather than at the center of a self-contained, private world. Walking invites us into a deeply physical knowing of the world and opens us to profound intimacy with God. The spiritual practice of walking patterns muscles and mind to discern the elusive traces of God in our world and in our lives. One aspect of Christian spirituality comes in discovering a mindful awareness of God in the immediacy of the present moment. The spiritual practice of walking nurtures this receptivity to God's presence in the here and now.

We do not have to walk through a nature preserve to experience this divine presence. One day in 1958, Trappist monk Thomas Merton was in downtown Louisville, Kentucky. He sat down on a bench at the corner of Fourth and Walnut and observed the people walking around him. In that moment at that busy intersection, Merton experienced an epiphany. He realized that all the people walking around him were not separate from him but were one with him and he was one with them. It felt like he had wakened from a dream of separateness.

Connecting Spirit, Mind, and Muscle

Walking as a spiritual practice results in a different quality of thought. Henry David Thoreau wrote that when his feet began to move, his thoughts began to flow. The Greek philosopher Diogenes supposedly said *solvitur ambulando*—"It is solved by walking." Walking helps us make connections. We can all remember at least one time when, frustrated by a seemingly insoluble problem, we took a walk to "clear our heads." And as we walked, the solution came to us. What are some implications of this relationship between muscles and mind for walking as a spiritual practice?

First, while we sometimes go for a walk with no specific destination in mind, most of the time we have a specific goal in mind when we set out. We are going from point A to point B. When we walk, then, we make physical connections between one place and another. In the same way, walking helps us make mental connections with ideas, feelings, hopes, or memories. Walking as a spiritual practice likewise helps us make connections between ourselves and God. Walking helps us recover the soul's hidden wholeness. It knits back together the fragmented and sometimes broken parts of the soul.

We do not have to think about walking. For most of us, our bodies mastered how to walk when we were toddlers. The point of walking is that we do not have to think about it. We just do it. Freed from the necessity of conscious thought, we can become mindfully present to the web of connections in which our lives are held in this present moment. These moments allow us to forge new mental connections. Walking as a spiritual practice moves us beyond our conscious minds so that we rediscover our many connections to God and to God's world.

Second, walking means traveling light. When I go for a long-distance walk, I never want more than twenty pounds in my backpack. A well-seasoned walker once taught me what he called the 20/80 rule: Carry no more than twenty pounds with you, even if it means taking only 80 percent of what you need. In the same way, walking as a spiritual practice means traveling light. If we feel burdened with too many fears, too much guilt and shame, or too many "oughts" and "shoulds," then we are unlikely to progress spiritually. Walking with Jesus means traveling light.

Third, because walking shapes the neural pathways of the mind, it affects our sense of self. When our two sons were born, their feet were inked and a nurse made imprints of the soles on their birth certificates. Their legal identity was forever linked to their feet. Could it be that the proof of who we are as children of God is in our feet?

One of my sons was born with a foot that turned inward. My wife and I feel blessed to live in a time when medical science could repair Jonathan's foot; we feel equally blessed to have access to health care resources that make such surgery possible. So a doctor surgically corrected Jonathan's tiny foot when he was six months old and now that grown man has walked to more places than we could ever have imagined possible when we brought him home from the hospital. He has hiked along Neolithic trade routes in southern England and the Loire Valley. He has sauntered along the streets of cities around the world. He has marched to protest injustice. His strong steps have steadied elderly relatives as they shuffled from hospital beds to kitchen tables. His feet have carried him forward to receive the body and blood of Christ in his cupped hands. Where Jonathan's feet have carried him cannot be separated from the person he has become.

If Jonathan had lived in a time when medical science could not repair his foot, his life and his sense of self would have differed greatly. His feet carry not only his physical weight but also his story and, therefore, his identity. Jonathan's feet are not merely physical appendages. They are an intimate part of a whole constellation of emotional, spiritual, and intellectual experiences that have shaped his personal and spiritual identity. Jonathan's experience is not unique. It holds true for everyone: Moving our soles sculpts our souls.

The Love of Speed and the Speed of Love

Fourteenth-century English mystic William Langland begins his *Piers the Plowman* by describing how, on a summer morning, when the sun was warm, he clothed himself in a shepherd's cloak and went out into the wide world searching for wonders. Langland goes on to describe the mystic visions of God that came to him on his travels. It all begins, however, when he steps out his door and goes for a walk on a warm summer day.

Living deeply has its own speed as does love. The poet John Keats wrote in a letter to a friend, "I have of late been moulting: not for fresh feathers and wings: they are gone, and in their stead I hope to have a pair of patient sublunary legs."[1] Is love's speed six hundred miles per hour? Perhaps it is three miles per hour. The Supremes' song "Can't Hurry Love" also applies to our relationship with God. When we willingly slow down to the pace of our patient sublunary legs, we discover a God who is already walking as our companion.

Our love of speed and our desire for convenience and comfort deaden our senses. Speed anesthetizes us to the world around us as well as to God, who walks with us. Dwelling inside climate-controlled spaces, inhabiting a virtual world of technological enhancements, the act of walking is a counter-cultural spiritual practice. We live in a world of comfort and convenience strongly influenced by our love of speed. Walking as a spiritual practice invites us to move at the speed of love.

A walking Jesus is a slow Jesus. Jesus' parables repeatedly suggest that God's reign will come slowly—like a little yeast that quietly works in the dough. It grows gradually until it has leavened the whole loaf. (Read Matthew 13:33.) The kingdom of God is like a mustard seed that silently takes root and slowly multiplies until it engulfs the whole field. (Read Matthew 13:31-32.)

The reign of God expands at a slow pace because it grows at the speed of love. Love takes time. God's reign, like walking, is slow. You cannot hurry it any more than you can hurry the unfolding of a rose's petals. Life unfolds from within. No technological enhancement or quick fix can speed its arrival.

Walking as a spiritual practice requires that we move atten- tively, receptively, mindfully through the present moment as if it were the only moment that matters because it is the moment in which we encounter the God who walks with us.

Walking Suggestions

I offer two walking suggestions for this week. You can employ these methods of walking meditation in a variety of settings: on a treadmill or in a natural setting, along a sidewalk or in a shopping mall. If you walk in a noisy location, consider using earplugs to deaden the sounds around you. If you walk with others, agree to chat with one another for the first few minutes, then give yourselves silent time to practice whatever method of walking meditation you are using. All these methods require that you leave your iPod at home. If you have a smartphone, be sure to turn it off or mute its sound.

Conscious Walking

All these methods rely on the body's physical sensations and innate rhythm as a means to focus the mind. The first method invites you to become aware of the movement of your body as you walk.

Before you begin your walk, gently stretch your muscles. Your hamstrings, calves, and thighs need a brief stretch to help increase your blood flow, balance, and coordination. As with all exercise, you should begin by stretching your muscles so they are warm; consequently, you'll be less apt to injure them as you walk.

Once you have finished stretching, stand in one place for a few moments and take three deep breaths, inhaling and exhaling slowly. Note the subtle shifts in your body as you stand with both feet on the ground. Notice how you are carrying your body and where you feel its weight.

Now begin walking. Do not try to hurry or walk quickly. Neither should you adopt a pace that feels abnormally slow. Just move at a normal pace.

Feel the spring in your heels and toes as you lift one foot into the air and bring the other one down to the ground. Experience the pull of the muscles in your feet, legs, and hips. Note how the muscles in your arms, shoulders, and neck are contracting and releasing as you swing your arms.

Give yourself over to the rhythm created by your feet. Do not try to go too slowly or too fast. Let the rhythm of your stride become a flow within you rather than a space between footfalls.

If thoughts or ideas come to mind, just let them float away. Do not focus on them. Simply return your focus to the sensation of your body as you walk. Do not make any judgments about your thoughts. Just observe them and let them go.

When you reach the end of your walk, come to a natural stop. Notice what it feels like to stand still. Press your feet to the floor or soil and ground yourself firmly in the here and now. Then gently stretch your muscles. Stretching is particularly important at the end of a walk. Notice what it feels like to stretch your muscles. Feel the tightness release itself.

Close with a prayer that captures the essence of your experience. A prayer might be this:

Loving God, you create me with a body that moves so that I may better serve you and others. I thank you for my body and especially for the gift of movement. You call me to walk many paths in my life. Some I have walked before. Others are unknown to me. Some I walk with others, and others I must walk alone. Give me faith to walk whatever path lies before me, always trusting that you walk beside me. Amen.

After your walk, write some notes in your walking journal about your experience.

Counting Your Strides

Begin with the stretching and breathing exercises outlined in the first Walking Suggestion.

As you walk, count your footsteps. You can count "one-two-three-four," repeating the sequence over and over. Once you have practiced this sequence, then try the following:

- Count your first seven steps ("one-two-three-four-five-six-seven").
- Then start over at one with your next step, and this time count to eight.
- With your next step, begin again at one and count to nine.
- Continue this pattern until your final number is "twelve."
- Then start the sequence again, beginning with seven and going up to twelve each cycle.

You can repeat this pattern as much as you would like. Again, the goal is simply to focus your mind on the rhythm of your steps. Let go of other thoughts or feelings that come to the surface. Bringing your mind back gently to your counting prevents you from focusing on your thoughts but instead creates an awareness of the here and now.

Conclude with the stretching exercises, prayers, and journaling outlined in the first Walking Suggestion.

Questions for Further Reflection

1. If you are a parent, do you remember your child's first steps? What do you recall about that moment? How did learning to walk change your child's life?

2. How many minutes do you walk each day? How much of your day do you spend sitting or standing rather than walking? (If you pursued the first Walking Suggestion in chapter 1, review your notes on how far and how much you walked last week.) Health and fitness researchers suggest that we aim for ten thousand steps per day. How close do you come? What would help you reach this goal?

3. When have you faced problems or issues that seemed difficult to resolve? Recall times when a solution unexpectedly came to you while you were taking a walk. What was this experience like? What does it suggest to you about walking as a spiritual practice?

4. Do you ever feel that your life is moving too fast? How do you personally slow down and bring God back into focus? Bring your own life back into focus?

5. How do you experience the love of speed and the speed of love in your life?

 ## three

Moving to a Larger Rhythm

During football season, my high school band performed at halftime shows and in parades. I always gave a sigh of relief when I finished marching band season. I could never march and play my instrument at the same time. It was like asking me simultaneously to pat my head and rub my stomach. One day, the band director became completely exasperated with me. "Hawkins, you have no sense of rhythm," he shouted. "You must be the only person in the world who plays to one beat and marches to another."

As an adult I decided to take piano lessons. My fingers coughed and sputtered as they moved over the keys. Finally, my piano teacher politely told that me I had no sense of rhythm. She described me as rhythmically impaired.

Life's most fundamental rhythms do not depend on drum majors or metronomes, however. All kinds of rhythms surround us: The sun rises and sets. The seasons come and go. We fall asleep and awaken to the body's circadian rhythm. The human heart contracts and relaxes rhythmically 60 to 100 times every minute; 100,000 times a day; 35 million times each year. We inhale and exhale 12 to 16 times each minute, 20,000 times each day. At the cellular level, the neurons that regulate our bodies fire to the rhythmic oscillation of electrochemical charges. These universal, interlocking rhythms extend from the smallest cells to the most distant galaxies. They affect all aspects of our lives.

A Matter of Life and Breath

When we walk, our feet also have a predictable rhythm. We walk to a constant one-two beat. Musicians call it a "duple meter" and it serves as the basis for many hymns and songs. Poets also know this duple-meter rhythm. English poetry's basic metrical unit that forms part of a line of verse is called a "foot." Poetry's earliest rhythms arose from the cadence of our walking feet. This relationship may explain why some of the greatest English-language poets were famous walkers. Scholars estimate that William Wordsworth walked 175,000 miles throughout his lifetime. Robert Frost and Wallace Stevens were both committed walkers.

This rhythmic cadence of our feet influences two other critical human rhythms: our heartbeat and our breathing. The energic cost of walking is increased oxygen consumption. The faster we walk, the more oxygen we need. The lungs respond by taking in more air, which places greater demand on the heart. So the heart rate increases accordingly. Thus, walking functions like a thermostat that regulates our breathing and our heart rate.

A comfortable alignment between breathing and walking is one breath to every three or four steps. If we sync the cadence of our steps to the cycle of our breathing, we tap into a channel of energy deep within the body. Breath, after all, is energy. Most of us normally take short, shallow breaths. We do not fully expand our diaphragms and fill our lungs. But when we walk, we tend to breathe more deeply, and our lungs and heart come in sync with the cadence of our footsteps. Walking trains our bodies to take deeper, slower breaths that better energize our bodies. Walking, we could say, is a matter of life and breath.

Walk, Breathe, Pray

How we breathe affects our physical performance. It also affects our spiritual performance. Most athletes recognize that breath is energy as do people who regularly engage in prayer and meditation.

Deep, regular breathing has a calming effect. When children cry, the first thing we say to them is, "Take a deep breath." As we breathe more deeply, our heart rate slows; we feel more calm, open, and relaxed. This slow, deep, regular breathing helps us achieve a mindful receptivity to God. Centering Prayer and other schools of meditation include an emphasis on deep, regular breathing. These methods typically suggest that we sit quietly and focus on our breathing. But we can also use the duple-meter rhythm of our feet to achieve the same deep breathing that fosters a mindful receptivity to God.

In the anonymous Russian spiritual classic *The Way of a Pilgrim*, a mendicant pilgrim describes his spiritual journey toward holiness. Responding to Paul's words to "pray without ceasing" (1 Thess. 5:17), the author wanders across Russia visiting monasteries and spiritual masters to learn how to pray without ceasing. The author describes himself as a homeless wanderer of humble beginnings who roams from place to place. He ultimately meets a *starets*, or venerated spiritual director, in a Russian Orthodox monastery who teaches him the Jesus Prayer ("Lord Jesus Christ, Son of God, have mercy on me, a sinner.") and advises him to repeat it six thousand times a day. His breathing governs these repetitions. He inhales at the name of Jesus and exhales as he pleads for mercy. When contemporary Christians are taught the Jesus Prayer, they learn to synchronize the words of the prayer with their breathing.

But what if the power of the Jesus Prayer ultimately relies more on how we walk than how we breathe? Our anonymous Russian pilgrim is not sitting in a monastery, staring at a candle, listening to chants, and breathing mindfully. He is walking. Constantly walking. He even walks across Russia to Siberia. The regular, duple-meter rhythm of his walking may serve as the underlying pattern that regulates his deep, rhythmic breathing. The cadence of the pilgrim's feet and the rhythm of his breathing echo the beating of his heart—a heart he continuously offers to God as his sacrifice of praise and thanksgiving.

The cadence of the pilgrim's feet is not incidental to his spiritual journey. Walking may be the unacknowledged energy that empowers his unceasing prayer of the heart. Can something so simple as walking foster a spirit of prayer and meditation? Why does this happen?

Breathing links our outer and inner worlds. The human lungs are the only internal organs exposed directly to the external environment. It is a huge exposure. If we were to unfurl the lungs, they would cover a surface area roughly the size of a tennis court. When we inhale, we draw the outer world into the very center of our bodies. When we exhale, we send something from the core of our being out into the world. The air that we exhale circulates through leaves and trees, enlivening them, only to be drawn back into someone else's lungs. The air we breathe has circulated all over the world. It has flowed through the lungs of a refugee in Syria, a truck driver in Asia, a scientist in Africa, a clarinet player in Austria, a child playing baseball in Denver. Our breathing links us to every other living thing on our planet.

The air we breathe has been around for a long time, cycling between lungs and leaves for thousands of years. When we inhale, we draw into the center of our bodies a vibrant connection to everything in God's beautiful, complex world. When we exhale, we give back to the world something that arises from the depths of our own being. Our awareness of this rhythm helps us recognize how our inner and outer realities are mutually interdependent.

No wonder the Hebrew word for spirit (*ruah*) also means breath and wind. "When you take away their breath, they die and return to their dust. When you send forth your spirit, they are created; and you renew the face of the ground" (Ps. 104:29-30).

We cannot separate the rhythm of our breathing from the duple-meter cadence of our feet. Each is entrained to the other. Both are synced to the beating of our hearts. For some people, sitting quietly and focusing on their breathing leads into a state of prayer. Others find it difficult to sit still. For them, the spiritual practice of walking provides an alternative pathway to the deep, rhythmic breathing that empties the mind of distractions and guides them to a mindful awareness of God's loving presence. This dynamic explains why Christian worship includes both moments of silence and movement, stillness and walking.

How Firm a Foundation

Our feet move through two phases as we walk: A stance or support phase and a swing phase. These two phases constitute its "duple meter" cadence. During the stance or support phase, we stiffen one leg and plant it solidly on the ground. This phase constitutes about 60 percent of the walking cycle. In the swing phase, we fling our other leg forward and let it drop, heel first, onto the ground ahead of us, which marks the initiation of another stance phase. We thus move along pendulum-like: One leg stiff and planted solidly on the ground; the other, swinging forward.

As we walk, we balance ourselves upright. This balance is never static but always dynamic. We are never fully "in balance" as we walk. We constantly move toward balance or away from it. Walking has been called a controlled fall forward.

This is the balance described in Ecclesiastes 3:1-8. "For everything there is a season, and a time for every matter under heaven," the poet begins. These verses then list a series of contrasts: a time to be born and a time to die, a time to weep and a time to laugh, a time to seek and a time to lose. These contrasts suggest the rhythmic balance of stance and swing. We seek and lose. We mourn and laugh. We embrace and let go.

In the 1870s, railroad baron, multimillionaire, and former California governor Leland Stanford took an interest in racehorses. At the time, a fierce debate existed over whether a trotting horse could simultaneously lift all four feet off the ground. Stanford wanted to establish the facts. The better he understood how horses trot, the better he could train a winning racehorse. So he hired Eadweard Muybridge, an English-born photographer, to determine conclusively whether or not trotting horses became airborne.

Muybridge's late-nineteenth-century cameras required motionless subjects to record an image. Photographic equipment did not have digital shutters and f-stops. You just took off the lens cap, exposed the photographic plate, waited a few moments, and then put the cap back in place. How could such equipment take pictures of a moving horse?

Muybridge came up with an ingenious solution. He placed a series of cameras along the racecourse. Each camera was attached to a wire stretched across the horse's path. As the horse moved down the track, it tripped a wire and the attached camera took a photograph of Stanford's horse. These photographs were then collated into a sequential, shot-by-shot view of the horse's feet. They proved that horses do indeed become airborne as they race down a track. Muybridge's technique was, in the end, as famous for laying the conceptual foundation for "moving pictures" as for adding to our understanding of how horses move their feet.

A human being is not a trotting horse, however. Human beings must always have at least one foot planted on ground. This is true whether we are walking a woodland trail or a spiritual path. At the end of the Sermon on the Mount, Jesus tells a parable. He describes two householders. One builds on sand, the other on rock. When the wind and rain come, the house built on sand gets swept away, but the one built on rock survives. The wise disciple receives Jesus' message and acts on it. "Everyone then who hears these words of mine and acts on them will be like a wise man who built his house on rock" (Matt. 7:24).

The solid spiritual foundation on which we plant our feet is the experience of God's grace at work in us, loving, forgiving, and healing us even when we feel unlovable or broken. Spiritual practices form the firm foundation that opens us to receive and cultivate God's grace in us. Fasting, spiritual reading, personal and corporate prayer, worship, examination of conscience, spiritual direction, and acts of service or mercy are all disciplines that ground us in the firm foundation of God's love. We usually call this firm footing a "rule of life." It is the pattern of spiritual disciplines to which we commit ourselves because we believe it provides a sound footing on which we can grow in the love, knowledge, and service of God.

When the Time Comes, Let It Go

The other 40 percent of walking's duple-meter stride is swinging our foot into the air and falling forward. To walk with Jesus requires embracing both balance and disequilibrium. It means discerning when to hold on and when to let go. Walking with Christ involves both stance and swing. We cannot stand forever, fixed on one foot. We have to risk letting go and falling forward into God's waiting arms.

Early in the twentieth century, the English explorer Ernest Shackleton set out to be the first person to cross Antarctica. It was a two thousand-mile trip through the planet's most extreme weather and inhospitable landscape. Shackleton and his crew failed to achieve their goal. Their ship, the *Endurance,* was trapped and crushed by ice in the Wendell Sea. Shackleton and his crew found themselves stranded twelve hundred miles from the nearest outpost of civilization.

When the ice broke up in the spring, the twenty-seven crew members launched three salvaged lifeboats and rowed toward Elephant Island, which was nothing more than an uninhabited rock surrounded by the sea. It was, however, the first solid ground under their feet in more than a year. On Elephant Island, Shackleton converted one of the lifeboats into a sailboat and with a hand-selected crew set out to sail for help through some of the stormiest waters on earth.

Seventeen days later, the crew landed on South Georgia Island, home to a small whaling station. Unfortunately, Shackleton and his companions had landed on the wrong side of the island. To reach the whaling station, they would have to walk thirty miles across a forty-five-hundred-foot mountain range. No one had ever made such a journey before. But Shackleton decided to cross the mountains. He and the crew reached the top of the ridge just as the sun was setting and the light fading. Gazing downward, they thought the slope might be safely navigated. But they could not be certain because conditions made it impossible to see that far below them.

Standing astride the ridgetop as darkness was falling and the fog was creeping higher, Shackleton asked his crew, "Can we stay here?" To stay on the ridgetop would mean certain death in the cold, fog, and darkness. His solution: They would sit on the ground in a single-file row, wrap their arms and legs around each other, and slide down the mountain like a toboggan team. His companions thought he had lost his mind. What if we hit a rock? Shackleton replied, "Can we stay here?" What if the slope turns into a cliff and we plunge over the edge? Shackleton replied, "Can we stay here?"

So, reluctantly, the men all sat down, wrapped their arms and legs together, and pushed off down the mountainside. Their descent took only a few, heart-stopping minutes. Then they began to slow down and finally came to a stop. They had descended the mountain without a single injury. Shackleton found help at the whaling station and then went back for the rest of the crew. Not a single crew member's life was lost.

Shackleton's voyage has become a legend of courage and leadership under extreme conditions. His question to his companions on the ridgetop is a question we all need to ask ourselves: Can we stay where we are? We need one foot on solid ground. But we cannot stay frozen in place forever. We have to swing forward, take risks, leave the past behind, and trust that God's waiting arms will embrace us. The Christian life is a path we walk, not a bucket of cement in which we plant our feet.

Letting Go and Stepping into God's Future

Letting go and falling forward is important soul-work. On the Mount of Transfiguration, Peter wants to build three shrines and stay forever on the mountaintop with Jesus, Elijah, and Moses. Like Shackleton and his crew, Jesus and his disciples are on a high mountain, straddling two choices: Stay or go? Jesus knows the answer to this question. Faithfulness to God sometimes means stepping beyond rock-solid truths, peering into the fog-covered valley below, and then trusting God enough to toboggan down the mountainside in the dark.

In an upper room on the night before Jesus' betrayal, he and his disciples celebrate the Passover meal. As they share the bread and cup, Jesus overturns the Passover's traditional meaning and invests it with a new significance. From now on, it will be a memorial of his broken body and blood. His disciples have already relinquished many of their religious certainties. They have listened to Jesus tell them, "You have heard it said to you; but now I say to you." (See Matthew 5:21-48.) Now Jesus asks his disciples to let go of their final certainty—the Passover. It will no longer recall the foundational event of their lives as faithful children of Israel, God's deliverance from slavery. From now on, it will recall Jesus' saving death on the cross. Jesus asks his disciples to let go of their religious upbringing's most dependable truth and step into a new, uncertain, and risky truth.

Letting go is hard to do. But sooner or later, we have to ask ourselves, "Can we stay here?" At one time or another in our lives, God calls us *not* to "remember the former things, or consider the things of old" because God is "about to do a new thing" (Isa. 43:18-19).

We maintain our spiritual balance only through the ongoing loss and recovery of a trustworthy center of gravity. Walking as a spiritual practice teaches us that we grow in Christ by entrusting ourselves to a continuous process of embrace and release, of holding on and letting go, of certainty and risk, of stance and swing. This wisdom is not abstract and theoretical but engraved in our muscle memory. We embody it physically on our soles before we know it in our souls.

Embodying Soul Experience in Our Soles

Not long ago I visited the Museum of Science and Industry in Chicago. One exhibit was called "YOU! The Experience." One particular display in its "Your Vitality" section intrigued me. Two people sit at opposite ends of a table. Each tries to make a ball roll from his or her end of the table toward the other side. Both wear around their heads a band equipped with sensors that monitor their alpha and theta brainwaves. These particular brainwaves occur when the brain is in a state of relaxation. So the goal is to out-relax one's opponent. The more you focus on mentally willing the ball to move away from you, the more it rolls toward you. Only when you let go and relax does the ball move in the direction you desire.

Most players (including me) find this a more daunting task than it would first appear to be. My natural tendency, when the ball comes rolling toward me, is to exert mental willpower to try to force it back toward my opponent's side of the table—the very thing that increases its movement toward me. The more I struggle mentally to control the direction of the ball, the less success I have. The more I let go and relax, the greater my success in having it roll toward my opponent. The player with the calmest mind rather than the one who exerts the most conscious willpower wins the game of Mindball.

In the same way, when I walk, I have to relax and let go of my need to control consciously my foot's movement in order to maintain my balance in the swing phase of my stride. If I think too consciously about willing my foot to move, I totter and stumble. If I try to will myself to stay in balance as my foot lifts and swings, I am more apt to feel off-kilter and fall. To walk smoothly and efficiently, I have to let go and almost effortlessly, semiautomatically follow my footfall's own forward movement. Walking and winning a game of Mindball share in common this ability to relax, to let go consciously of willing something to happen in order to reach a goal. Walking as a form of meditation can move us beyond our need to control our lives through heroic self-exertion.

Paul suggests that the root of the human dilemma resides in our sense of life's precariousness, which prompts us to try to secure our lives through our own willpower and self-assertion rather than to trust in the goodness of a gracious God to sustain our lives no matter our circumstances. But these efforts do not resolve our basic human dilemma; they only intensify our basic problem, which is itself our need to control, to pre-empt for ourselves what belongs to God alone. The more we attempt to please God through our own achievements and accomplishments, the more our fundamental sense of insecurity and inadequacy increases. Paul thus invites us to let go of our willful efforts to control the worth and meaning of our lives and instead to accept God's gracious acceptance of us. (Read Romans 3:20; 4:1-5; 5:12-21.) We can then rejoice in the life God gives us and deploy the energy we have tied up in our fruitless self-exertion and self-promotion by experiencing and rejoicing in the fullness of life to which God calls us.

Sometimes I have been driving on an icy road and my car will go into a skid. As I feel the car sliding off the road, I instinctively try harder to steer the car in the direction I want it to go, turning the wheels away from the skid and back onto the road. Yet this effort is useless. To regain control of the car, I have to let go of my efforts to control the skid by fighting against it. Instead I have to steer into the skid and let the vehicle move with it. Then and only then, do I have an opportunity to redirect the car onto the road. I must yield to and work with the energy of the skid rather than fight against it. Our excessive focus on the ability to grasp, to control, and to manage our lives by willpower and self-exertion similarly causes us to push harder in areas of our lives where exertion and striving prove profoundly counterproductive.

Walking as a spiritual practice engenders the capacity to trust, to yield ourselves, and to let go, which can cultivate in us a deep, God-given "body thinking." This body thinking responds to the present moment and knows when to hold a

stance and when to swing forward. Walking as a spiritual practice teaches us that letting go is not the same thing as being
passive. Together, the stance and swing phases of our walking
stride represent an invitation to move beyond our usual mental categories of being active or passive, of attachment and
detachment.

We walk by cooperating with the flow of the moment.
We are neither passive nor "making it happen" by intentional,
conscious effort. We best describe the truth of Christian life
as responsiveness to God's Spirit, which requires of us stillness
and movement, holding on and letting go as the Spirit wills.
For the Spirit blows where it wills and we cannot control or
direct it through our own efforts. (Read John 3:8.)

Walking requires that we entrust ourselves to a moving
yet still balance point within ourselves rather than believe we
achieve a life pleasing to God through our own self-exertion
and willpower. To walk as disciples of Jesus Christ means being
responsive *to* and taking responsibility *for* the present moment
in which God comes to us, speaks to us, and calls us forth to
new life.

Slippery Slopes and Stumbling Blocks

The spiritual practice of walking involves more than moving
to the rhythm of stance and swing. Walkers occasionally slip on
a wet sidewalk or trip over a tree root. Pilgrims occasionally
fall down or lose their way. What does the spiritual practice of
walking have to say about these experiences? To answer this
question, consider the difference between a trip and a slip.

I slip due to insufficient friction between the sole of my shoe and the surface beneath it. I stiffen my leg in the stance phase and put my weight on it. Then I discover that this surface is unstable and slippery: a wet leaf, an invisible layer of ice, a thin film of water on the floor. A slip happens in the stance phase of my stride. I slip because my foot has not made solid contact with the surface beneath it. A slip usually means that I fall backward.

Spiritually, we slip when we shift our focus away from God. In Psalm 73, the author looks away from God and turns his or her gaze to the arrogant who scoff at God and wear pride as a necklace. The arrogant have sleek, sound bodies and prosper in all they do. Looking at their success rather than at God, the psalmist almost loses faith in the Lord. Then the poet enters the sanctuary and looks upon God in the beauty of holiness. And the perspective shifts: "You hold my right hand. You guide me with your counsel. . . . Whom have I in heaven but you? And there is nothing on earth that I desire other than you" (vv. 23-25). As for those evildoers, they are the ones whose feet are about to slip: "Truly you set them in slippery places; you make them fall to ruin" (v. 18).

When we slip spiritually, we have shifted our gaze away from God and focused it on someone or something else. When we turn back and gaze once more on God in the beauty of holiness, we find solid ground beneath our feet. The faithful practice of spiritual disciplines brings God's presence, power, and purposes into clear focus. It centers us in God so that the eyes of our hearts do not shift their focus elsewhere and lead us onto a slippery slope.

We are commonly advised to "walk like a penguin" on an icy parking lot or sidewalk. While we naturally tend to move our feet closer together as we tiptoe along, we need instead to spread our legs farther apart and point our feet outward. This physical stance lowers our center of gravity and gives us greater stability. In the same way, when we feel that we might be slipping spiritually, we need to broaden our stance, not narrow it. We need to broaden our connections of support and accountability, not withdraw from Christian community. Instead of reducing the time we spend in prayer and listening for God, we need to "walk like a penguin" and expand the ways in which we attend to the means of grace.

A trip differs from a slip. We trip in the swing phase of our stride, not during the stance phase. When I trip, I have swung my foot forward only to have it catch itself on a tree root, an uneven spot in the path, or a piece of concrete thrust upward from the sidewalk. I trip when the forward thrust of my foot during the swing phase meets an object that interferes with its movement. When I slip, I fall backward; but when I trip, I typically fall forward.

The people of the Bible largely traveled on rocky, uneven trackways. Travelers could easily trip over a stone or uneven spot. Jeremiah draws on a common, everyday experience when he has God announce, "I am laying before this people stumbling blocks against which they shall stumble" (Jer. 6:21).

I usually trip or stumble when I am in a hurry. We can also trip when we are in a hurry to grow spiritually. Looking for quick and painless spiritual growth, we end up taking short-cuts that undermine our growth. We become impatient with ourselves, others, and God. This impatience eventually trans-forms itself into frustration and anger with God.

The Bible also describes stumbling or tripping as some-thing that happens "in the dark." We can trip spiritually over the occult, the magical, or signs and wonders that bedazzle us. Our busyness in looking for signs, wonders, and extraordinary spiritual experiences causes us to miss God's activity right here, right now.

Each of the Synoptic Gospels refers to Psalm 118:22, "The stone that the builders rejected has become the chief corner-stone." (See Matthew 21:42; Mark 12:10; Luke 20:17.) That cornerstone, Jesus, became a stumbling block to the religious authorities. Their presuppositions and assumptions about who the Messiah would be blinded them. Sometimes we trip spir-itually because we have fixed, rigid assumptions about God. The spiritual practice of walking invites us to examine our presuppositions and assumptions and to ask how they may be stumbling blocks to a more intimate walk with God.

What is the cure for tripping or slipping? Even Peter stum-bled and fell, and Jesus walked right beside him. The most faith-ful response comes in getting back up, learning from our bruises and scrapes, and then finding our way back onto the path. No matter how many times we trip or slip, God promises to lift us up and set us once more on the right path. God leads us in right paths for God's name's sake. Even though we walk through the darkest valley, God is with us, comforting us and anointing our scraped knees or elbows with oil. We trust that "goodness and mercy shall follow [us] all the days of [our] life" (Ps. 23:6).

Walking as a spiritual discipline teaches us to slow down and pay attention to the direction our feet are pointing and to the foundations on which we are building our spiritual lives. It also equips us to take the risk of stepping out in faith even when the path seems darkest. For someone who remains hurried and risk-averse, this is difficult advice and a hard discipline. But paying attention prepares us to walk faithfully as a disciple of Jesus Christ.

Walking Suggestions

Just as walking has a rhythm, so does breathing. The walking suggestions for this week invite us to explore ways we can synchronize these two rhythms so that we slow down and pay attention to what we are experiencing within us and around us in deeper, more mindful ways.

Counting Your Breaths

After a short warm-up walk, loosen your body and begin walking at a pace that is about average for you.

Imagine that every time you exhale, your breath is flowing out of your body in a gentle arc. As you inhale, envision your breath looping back into you. Make the circle of inhaling and exhaling as seamless as possible. Keep your breaths deep and even so that each one lasts about the same length of time. Once you have a deep, regular pattern of breathing, try to bring your breathing into rhythm with your steps. You could count "in-two-three-four" and "out-two-three-four." If your in-and-out rhythm becomes uneven, start again.

You can replace the "in/out-two-three-four" with a brief verse from the Bible. Choose a scripture or hymn passage no more than about seven or eight syllables long. Let the rhythm of your words, your breathing, and your steps flow into one rhythm as much as possible. Do not expect this to happen on your first try. It takes time and practice to bring your breathing into rhythm with your stride.

Another possible method is to use the Jesus Prayer ("Lord Jesus Christ, Son of God, have mercy on me, a sinner"). Other walkers write their own "breath" prayer. To do this:

- Pick an image of God that speaks to you.
- Identify what it is you wish to give to God or need from God. Then summarize this offering of praise, petition, or intercession in a short phrase.
- Combine the phrase that contains an image of God with your other phrase into a line that contains no more than seven or eight syllables. This becomes your own breath prayer. You inhale deeply and slowly on the first three or four syllables and then exhale deeply and slowly on the remaining ones. Your personal breath prayer might go like this: "Jesus, Lamb of God, heal my heart." Or "Lord of history, bring us peace."

When you finish, take some deep breaths and stretch. Afterward, you may wish to make notes about your experience: What was hard? easy? What was happening physically to you? Where did the rhythm take you spiritually?

Walking to a Musical Beat

Rather than counting, repeating a scripture verse, or using a breath prayer, select a simple refrain from a hymn or chorus that you find meaningful. Be sure to pick something with a four-four or two-four beat. Do not select a three-four beat that resembles a waltz.

Begin with the stretching and breathing exercises outlined in the first Walking Suggestion.

As you walk, repeat mentally the refrain or chorus to the rhythm of your footsteps. The objective is to sync the rhythm of your stride with the words of the refrain. If you have thoughts that arise, let them go and bring your mind back to the refrain. You are centering your spirit and creating a free, open space that is receptive to God.

Conclude with the stretching exercises, prayers, and journaling outlined in the first Walking Suggestion.

Questions for Further Reflection

1. What spiritual disciplines provide you with solid ground for your walk with Jesus?

2. When have you had to let go of a belief, value, or behavior that once served you well but later became a barrier to your spiritual well-being or growth?

3. What do you need to let go of in order to find balance in your Christian life?

4. Are you more likely to slip or trip in your Christian life? How does the distinction between slipping and tripping help you clarify your answer?

5. How would you evaluate your degree of resilience? When you slip or trip spiritually, how long does it take you to get back on your feet and start moving again? What supports your resilience? What barriers get in the way?

Keep track of the various cadences and rhythms you have around you each day (don't forget the ticking of the clock on the wall). How many do you count? Which ones exist in the natural world? Which ones are mechanical? How do they vary in pace? volume? How do these rhythms have a positive or a negative impact on your walk with Christ?

 four

On the Road

Just outside the kitchen door at my house sits a ten-gallon earthenware jar. My grandmother made pickles in it. It now holds walking sticks, not pickles. A long, slender walking stick towers above the others. My grandfather always took that same walking stick when we walked in the woods hunting for mushrooms in the spring. I now take it with me when I look for mushrooms in those same spots. Another stick is thick and stubby. Made of hickory, it belonged to my father. The bark has developed a red patina where hands have gripped it across two lifetimes. Still other walking sticks are child-sized, cut long ago for my now adult sons.

Which stick I pull from the jar depends on my mood, the time of year, or where I imagine my feet will take me. I usually go across the pasture and follow an old farm lane that snakes uphill through the woods. Eventually it crosses a railroad right-of-way and empties into a river bottom where my family grows corn and soybeans.

My grandmother, who lived to be 103 years old, remembered riding in a Model-T on this old road. As a young woman she traveled the road when she visited her relatives—the Woodyards—who lived in a log cabin at the top of the ridge. The log cabin vanished several generations ago. Only a stone-lined well and some daffodils that bloom in the spring remain as mute witnesses to the Woodyards and their home at the top of the ridge.

Its sinuous path suggests that the road began as an animal trackway. Between its life as a trackway and its years as a graveled road to the Woodyards' home, it probably existed as a dirt path along which horses pulled farm equipment between the pasture and the river bottom. Old stumps and fallen tree crowns indicate that it may also have served as a timber road along which loggers carried logs to market. Today the road has reverted to its original purpose—a trackway for deer, coyotes, raccoons, or an occasional fox. And, of course, a woodland rambler like myself.

Like my jar of walking sticks, old roads are also containers. They contain the record of all who have ever walked them. They provide a repository of meaning and memory.

Streets as Strata of Meaning and Memory

The English word *street* derives from an Indo-European root shared with words like *strata* or even *streusel*. It refers to something that is spread or stretched out in layers over a surface. Geologically, *strata* refers to different layers of sedimentary stone that lie atop one another. We see them as the bands of differently colored rock in a cliff or road cut. In cooking, a strata is a casserole-like dish that we make by layering different ingredients.

Like casseroles and sedimentary rock formations, roads are also multilayered. Highway contractors build roads in a layer-like fashion. After removing the topsoil, they establish a capping layer and subbase. Next they pour and roll several layers of asphalt to form a smooth, impermeable surface. Roads are, quite literally, layers of different materials put down in a specific sequence.

To a historian, roads reflect different strata of human occupancy. My old road served as an animal trackway before European settlers arrived in the 1830s. It later became a dirt path for farmers and their horses. The advent of automobiles brought a gravel surface, and the Woodyards built a house along it. With the decline of small-scale farming, the house and farm were abandoned and the road reverted to an animal trackway.

Ancient manuscripts share something in common with roads, sedimentary rocks, and casseroles. They too can have distinct strata. Scribes preferred to write on parchment rather than papyrus or paper. But turning animal hides into parchment was an expensive process. So, to make the best use of a valuable resource, scribes would sometimes scrub earlier text from a parchment page and write a new text on it. No scrubbing was ever perfect, however. So faint traces of the older text could remain visible beneath the more recent one. Scholars call these parchment sheets palimpsests.

Lost classical texts or alternate readings of biblical passages have been recovered from palimpsests. In 1998, an anonymous collector bought a medieval prayer book at an auction and donated it to the Walters Art Museum in Baltimore, Maryland. It was a palimpsest. Medieval monks, having less interest in mathematical theorems, had scrubbed the works of Archimedes off the parchment pages and copied their prayers onto them. Fortunately the monks did not do a thorough scrubbing. Beneath the text of this thirteenth-century prayer book scholars discovered the only known copies of Archimedes's *The Method of Mechanical Theorems* and his *Stomachion.*

Like a palimpsest, a road preserves layers of memory and meaning. Every October, my grandfather and I walked a path near our home to look for bittersweet vines. We would clip off branches laden with bright orange and red berries and carry them home. My grandmother would weave them into a Thanksgiving wreath for her front door. Many years later, I walked the same road with my sons. We would bring home bittersweet from the same vines and weave it into a wreath for our door. My adult sons now live far from home. Yet I still walk this path each October and look for bittersweet. My walk is a palimpsest. Beneath my feet are the layered footprints of four generations who have walked this same way on autumn days to gather bittersweet.

The road through my woods is also a palimpsest, as are some city sidewalks that I have walked for most of my adult life. So are ancient pathways and trading routes. As I travel along them, I walk through layers of time and memory.

The Way That Leads to Life

The Hebrew word *derek* (*drk*), which means "road" or "way" occurs more than seven hundred times in the Old Testament. Then as now, roads formed society's circulatory system. Goods, peoples, ideas, and armies moved along roads. As a land bridge among Asia, Africa, and Europe, ancient Palestine was crisscrossed with international highways, regional roads, and local trails. Most were very rudimentary, even the royal highways. Building a road consisted of little more than clearing away the vegetation and moving the bigger stones aside. (See Isaiah 62:10; 40:3; 57:14; Jeremiah 18:15.) The two most important international routes were The King's Highway and The Way of the Sea.

The King's Highway followed a north-south route and passed to the east of the Jordan River. Few cities or forts existed along it. Nomadic caravans used it to travel between Arabia and Damascus. It was little more than a trail for shepherds and their flocks. It is nonetheless a palimpsest of journeys and encounters. Abraham traveled it to pursue local kings who had abducted his nephew, Lot. (See Genesis 14.) Moses petitioned the king of Edom and Sihon, an Amorite king of Heshbon, to pass along it on the way to the Promised Land. (See Numbers 20:14-18; 21:21-26.) Their refusal prompted a confrontation in which God came to the aid of the wandering children of Israel.

The Way of the Sea stretched along the Mediterranean coast and possessed major military and economic significance. Ancient Egyptian documents refer to it, as do Assyrian and

Babylonian records. Like the King's Highway, the Way of the Sea is a palimpsest. Some of the Bible's most famous battles were fought along it. King Josiah was killed there while fighting Pharaoh's army near Meggido. (See 2 Kings 23:29.) The prophet Isaiah may draw on ancient memories of the Way of the Sea in his prophecy of King Hezekiah's accession to the Judean throne. (See Isaiah 9:2-7.) Centuries later, Matthew quotes Isaiah's words in his narrative of Jesus' birth. (See 4:12-16.) Every Advent, Christians across the globe who have never set foot on the Way of the Sea still repeat its name as they hear once more that light has dawned for a people who sat in deep darkness and the shadow of death.

Traders, travelers, pilgrims, and soldiers also traversed smaller regional roads and local trails. The Bible refers to literally hundreds of these byways. Genesis 35:19 and 48:7, for example, mention the Way of Ephrath, which runs near Bethlehem. The Way of Atharim extended from Kadesh-Barnea to Arad. (See Numbers 21:1.) Judges 8 mentions the Way of the Tent Dwellers and Judges 9:37 describes a local trail known as the Way of the Diviners' Oak located near Shechem.

Worshipers traveled these same roads on their way to Jerusalem for its pilgrim feasts. They sang from a collection of psalms as they walked. We still sing and pray these same Psalms of Ascent (120–134) Nomads herded their flocks along these roads. Traders transported goods and wares over them. Kings depended on them to move troops into war zones. They are palimpsests of Israel's history.

These roads are far more than physical realities; they are multilayered spiritual spaces invoked by prophets, poets, and sages. The Hebrew word *derek* does not simply describe a route between two points on a map. It defines a way of living in relationship to God. Moses warns the children of Israel, "I know that after my death you will surely act corruptly, turning aside from the way (*drk*) that I have commanded you." Moses means both a literal, physical road and a particular mode of conduct and a disposition of the heart.

The psalmists similarly invite worshipers to meditate on how God teaches the humble to walk in God's way [*drk*]. (Read Psalm 25:9, 12.) The author of Psalm 139 pleads for God to "lead me in the way [*drk*] everlasting" (v. 24). The prophet Jeremiah envisions a day when God will establish a new covenant with God's people. It will be a new way of walking with God in singleness of heart: "They shall be my people, and I will be their God. I will give them one heart and one way [*drk*], that they may fear me for all time, for their own good and the good of their children after them. I will make an everlasting covenant with them" (Jer. 32:38-40).

New Testament Road Trips with Jesus

The Greek New Testament translates *derek* with the word *hodos*, which also means "way" or "road." *Hodos* occurs about ninety times in the New Testament. One-half of these usages occur in Luke-Acts. Almost all of them are figurative uses. At least six times in the Acts of the Apostles, Luke uses *hodos* as the title of the early Christian movement. (See Acts 9:2; 19:9, 23; 22:4; 24:14, 22.) Discipleship, according to Luke-Acts, means walking a certain Way or path.

Like *derek* and *hodos*, the English word *way* has several literal and figurative meanings. It can refer to a real, physical road that connects one place to another. It can also mean the method or means we use to travel a road, as in "I need a way to get to church next Sunday." In still other settings, it can mean how we act, behave, or do our work ("He has his own way of baking the Communion bread.")

When Luke describes the early Christians as followers of the Way, he simultaneously invokes all these meanings. (See Acts 9:2; 18:25; 19:9; 22:4; 24:14; 24:22.) Walking with Jesus moves us from one place in life to another: from brokenness to wholeness, for example. But it also prescribes a particular method or mode of conduct and behavior. This meaning, after all, is the original sense in which John Wesley's followers were called "Methodists." Thus, in Luke 20:20-21, the scribes and chief priests say to Jesus, "Teacher, we know that you are right in what you say and teach, and you show deference to no one, but teach the way (*hodos*) of God in accordance with truth." They do not mean that Jesus teaches people the best roads to travel on their way to the Temple. They mean Jesus teaches a way of life that is faithful to God's will.

Luke organizes a large section of his Gospel as a "road trip" or travel narrative. Luke's *hodos* narrative resembles modern road-trip literature such as John Steinbeck's *Travels with Charley* or William Least Heat-Moon's *Blue Highways*. Like these authors, Luke's narrative is less about the physical trip than what the author learns along the way.

Luke's travel narrative includes pivotal stories of spiritual transformation that happen on roads and pathways: (1) Paul's conversion on the road to Damascus; (2) the disciples' encounter with the risen Christ on the Emmaus road; (3) Philip's conversion of the Ethiopian eunuch on the road to Gaza; (4) Jesus' roadside invitation to Zacchaeus; (5) his call to Peter, James, and John as he walks along a shoreline path; and (6) his healing of the blind man who calls to him from the roadside. Some of Luke's most memorable parables also happen along a road. Both the parable of the good Samaritan and the parable of the prodigal son describe spiritual transformations that occur when people take to the road.

Roads as Thin Places

Friends of mine sometimes describe a retreat center, religious shrine, or chapel as a "thin place." Others return repeatedly to a special beach, lake, or place of natural beauty because it is a "thin place." In calling each location a thin place, they are saying that this spot has become a place where they experience God's presence more intensely. Like the thin layers of soil and memory that have built up along a woodland road or railroad track or the thin layers of ink and image on a palimpsest, persons experience certain physical locations as where the overlay of the human, natural, and divine realities is particularly thin.

For a long time, I thought of pilgrimage paths, the Stations of the Cross, or other places in the physical landscape in this way. They were, for me, "thin places" where I could sometimes experience this palimpsest-like connection with God and God's people across time and space.

I have gradually come to realize, however, that a road's physical landscape does not make it a thin place. Thin places, in fact, have ceased to be places at all in the conventional sense. A road's physical landscape—not even that of a pilgrim way hallowed by centuries of use—does not make it a "thin place." Thin places are ultimately those moments of relationship and mutuality with the strangers we meet when we are on these journeys. In some mysterious way, the strangers we meet along the way become the Christ whom scripture tells us often comes in the stranger's guise.

Roads are where we cross boundaries. They allow strangers to meet on the level ground of mutuality and vulnerability, care and openness. In these very encounters, we experience God coming to us and calling us forth to new journeys.

This palimpsest-like feeling of walking simultaneously through multiple layers of time and experience is not, of course, limited to walking the way of the cross or traveling a pilgrim pathway. It is essentially the same experience we have when we gather around the Lord's Table for Holy Communion. As we receive, bless, break, and share the bread and cup, we are gathered in a specific time and place and among a particular people. But we are also gathered around a table in an upper room in Jerusalem on the night long ago when Jesus was betrayed and simultaneously lifted up into the presence of all the saints at God's heavenly table.

In a certain sense, then, every road or path is a palimpsest, a "thin place," because every road or path potentially leads to a thoroughfare encounter with Jesus. Roads are palimpsests where we may glimpse another Way beneath, behind, or beyond this one. Walking as a spiritual practice trains us to recognize these palimpsests of the Spirit as we walk life's paths.

I once made a retreat at a convent near St. Louis. Early each morning, I walked a path that led me along outdoor Stations of the Cross that invited me to pause, reflect, and pray at each station. Walking them transported me back to first-century Jerusalem where I accompanied Jesus on his Way of Sorrows. I had stepped back in time to Jerusalem, and I was walking the Via Dolorosa with Jesus. These Stations of the Cross also invited me to step into the dark passageways of prison cells and torture chambers around the world where prisoners of conscience suffer and die. Jesus still walks with them on the Via Dolorosa. To walk these Stations of the Cross was, for me, to step into a palimpsest where time and space collapsed and I simultaneously stepped through multiple layers of memory and experience in a world where all points and places are equidistant in God.

Roads as Places of Encounter and Transformation

First-century Greek religion regarded space as sacred. So temples and shrines were "thin places" where a worshiper came to meet the gods and make sacrifices. The early Christians largely rejected this notion of sacred space. Instead, they spoke of a Way—something movable and not fixed in geography or physical space. The earliest Christians gathered in homes, by the river, outside the gates, along the road. The earliest traditions of Israel likewise suggested that people meet and come to know God on the way. God encounters Jacob in a dream as he stops by the roadside to sleep. Moses accompanies his flock on a Bedouin trail when God calls to him from the burning bush. The children of Israel do not have a fixed sacred shrine in the wilderness. They have a portable tent of meeting that moves with them. The prophets remind Israel repeatedly that God does not dwell in a house built by human hands but fills the whole creation. (See 2 Samuel 7:5-7; Isaiah 66:1; Acts 7:46.)

An authentic thin place for me is therefore a relationship, not a place. It is a moment of encounter and mutuality, vulnerability and compassion that unexpectedly intrudes when I am on my way somewhere and least expect a divine intrusion into my life. Every road that we walk holds the potential to become a "thin place." Streets and roads are public ways open to all sorts of people. When we go for a walk, we have to be ready to jostle elbows with strangers whom we might otherwise keep at arms' length. Streets and sidewalks are boundary-crossings where we encounter strangers and discover new truths. "Do not neglect to show hospitality to strangers, for by doing that some have entertained angels without knowing it" (Heb. 13:2).

I once stayed at a retreat center near downtown Chicago for a workshop. At the end of each afternoon's session, I took a long walk through city streets and neighborhoods to get my body moving and to clear my thoughts. All kinds of folks filled the crowded streets. One afternoon, I saw a man walking toward me. He was dressed shabbily and was talking loudly to himself. Pedestrians around me immediately crossed the street to avoid him. They believed him to be mentally ill or on drugs. As the man approached, I realized that everyone else had crossed to the other side. I was the only one who remained on his side of the street. Our eyes met, and I automatically said, "God bless you." He looked at me with a startled expression and replied, "God bless you too."

Each of us kept walking. Did my acknowledging him as just another person on the sidewalk rather than as a potentially dangerous stranger cause some shift in him, however slight? Did my words of blessing make any difference in his life? Was this encounter meant to change my perception of strangers? How did the meeting make me more accepting, more compassionate? Was it a thoroughfare transformation like those described in Luke's Gospel? Did I encounter an angel without knowing it as I went out for my evening walk? And what announcement did this angel make?

In Nazareth, churches are built over two spots, each claiming to be the site of the Annunciation. The Roman Catholic Basilica of the Annunciation is supposedly built over Mary's home. It assumes that the angel Gabriel visited Mary in her home to tell her the glad tidings that she would bear the son of God. A few streets away, another church is built over what Orthodox believers regard as the site of the Annunciation. This site encloses a spring from which water still flows into the church and a nearby well. Orthodox believers assume that Mary had stepped out onto the street to draw water from the neighborhood well when the angel Gabriel appeared to her. The Basilica of the Annunciation is grand and inspiring, but I preferred the Orthodox site when I visited Nazareth.

According to this tradition, the Annunciation was a thorough-fare encounter.

Angelic annunciations can happen anywhere. For me, they typically happen "on the way" when I have stepped out of the safety of my private world and entered into public spaces. Like an afternoon walk on a Chicago street. They come often as interruptions and unanticipated disruptions when I am "on the way" somewhere. They open up a palimpsest-like place in my life where I encounter God's presence and purposes in my life. We cannot contrive or force annuncia-tions. Not every encounter results in a spiritual transforma-tion. But each one carries the potential to disorient us, to confuse the artificial categories that we create to make the world more predictable or manageable. Being on the Way can jolt us out of ordinary ways of thinking, seeing, and respond-ing to others. Stepping onto the Way means being willing to share our stories, to talk about the real issues of our lives, and to listen with undivided attention to other people's deepest truths. Who knows, in such moments we may be entertaining angels without knowing it.

Persevering on the Path Set before Us

Stepping out of our safe, private worlds onto the Way of Jesus Christ is not easy. Welcoming strangers, embracing differences, and living with ambiguity or uncertainty is never easy. It can transform us much as Jesus transformed Zacchaeus when they met on the road. Jesus calls it a narrow way and contrasts it with the broad path that promises a safer, easier journey. (Read

Matthew 7:13-14.) The Way of Jesus is narrow because it is the way of suffering love, vulnerability, and receptivity that becomes a way of peace and joy.

It takes perseverance to walk with Jesus. The Way of Christ is not a path we walk for a few days or weeks but a way of life for life. In 1 Corinthians 9:24-27, Paul compares it to a foot-race that requires discipline and training. I have a friend who walks in fund-raising half-marathons together with his spouse. They are always training for the next event. They go out every morning, rain or shine, and walk at least two hours. Sometimes I think that they exercise greater discipline in their marathon training than I do in my practice of prayer.

Perseverance means finding a sustainable pace. I generally walk at a brisk pace but I am not trying to power walk. Sometimes a cluster of walkers will blast past me. Later, I overtake them by the wayside where they have stopped to catch their breath. In the same way, I have known seekers who decided to "fix" their spiritual lives. They have great enthusiasm and usually adopt several Christian disciplines all at once. If one practice is good for the soul, then ten must be even better. Typically, they bite off more than they can chew. In the end, they feel overwhelmed and defeated.

I frequently counsel people to pick no more than one or two Christian practices to integrate into their lives at any one time. When we set reasonable goals for ourselves, we are less subject to burnout and a loss of focus. If we are to persevere in the Christian Way, we need to remember it is a long-distance journey and not a one-hundred-yard sprint.

Staying the course is an obvious part of perseverance both for walkers and for disciples of Jesus Christ. When I walk long distances, there comes an inevitable moment when I hit the wall. The end of the trail seems a long way off, and I am ready to quit. Maybe I can call a cab that will take me to a nearby bed-and-breakfast where I can take a hot bath and burrow into a comfortable bed. To walk with Jesus requires a commitment to keep to the path, even when our feet hurt. "As they were going along the road. . . . Another said, 'I will follow you, Lord; but let me first say farewell to those at my home.' Jesus said to him, 'No one who puts a hand to the plow and looks back is fit for the kingdom of God'" (Luke 9:57, 61-62).

My son Jonathan and I were once walking one of England's national trails. On our third day, we walked along a badly rutted and uneven section of chalk road. Jonathan twisted his ankle. That night, I was ready to stop, not wanting to see Jonathan make his ankle worse. Jonathan, however, insisted that we keep walking. He wrapped his ankle in a bandage and kept going. The next day proved to be the best day of our trip. Yes, Jonathan was limping. But we would have missed the skylarks soaring above us. We would never have rested under ancient Sarsen stones for lunch and met some inspiring schoolteachers who were taking their students on an outing. Jonathan's perseverance was rewarded by a great day of walking that we both remember. (Although he also regretted my overly anxious concern about his ankle!). The rewards for perseverance on the Way of Christ are not just the wonders of heaven that meet us at the end of the road. They are also the transformative thoroughfare encounters we experience along the way.

Never Walk Alone

We persevere best when we travel the way with other pilgrims who can encourage us and hold us accountable. One of the primary rules for walking is never to travel alone.

A few years ago I attempted to hike part of the Pennine Way that runs from the Scottish border to the Peak District National Park in England. I was walking alone, and I planned to cover the fourteen miles from Baldersdale to Keld. When I reached Sleightholme Moor, I unfortunately lost the main path completely as I crossed a seemingly endless quagmire of wet, boggy peat marsh—exactly what I had always envisioned when I heard the word *moor*. The bleak landscape featured not a single sheep, cow, or abandoned stone hut.

Then it began to rain. The wind picked up speed. The fog settled around me. With all my leapfrogging from grassy tussock to tussock, I lost sight of trail markers. Nor could I find the usual muddy boot prints that indicated the passage of other hikers along the same path. Finally I sat down on a rock. I had never felt so wet, lost, and alone in such a seemingly godforsaken place. Hypothermia could easily set in given the conditions. I swallowed back my own sense of panic.

Then, out of nowhere, I heard the clank of pots and pans. I could see no one in the rain and fog around me. But I shouted a loud hello, and two long-distance hikers responded. They had something that I lacked: GPS and a more detailed Ordnance Survey map. More importantly, the two of them were traveling together while I was hiking alone. In the fog and on a poorly marked trail, two heads are always better than one.

I gratefully joined them, and together we made our way to a youth hostel in Keld. After that day on the Pennine Way, I decided never again to hike alone. Any walk, especially a long-distance one, harbors unknown dangers.

Walking alone is dangerous. Anything can happen on a trail. We can get injured and have no one to send for help. We need companions in Christ who will walk with us. In Luke's travel narrative, Jesus sends his disciples ahead of him in pairs. They do not travel alone. When Jonathan twisted his ankle, I lightened his steps by carrying his backpack as well as my own. He needed someone to bear his burden so he could keep going. Companions in Christ help us carry our burdens so we can continue together on the Way.

We also need the accountability of someone who says, "Are you sure you want to go that way?" when we decide to take a shortcut. Small groups, particularly covenant discipleship groups, provide the supportive accountability we need to stay on the Way. A trusted spiritual friend can offer similar support. Some people discover that meeting regularly with a spiritual director keeps them on the right path. Walking as a spiritual practice reminds us that the Christian life is not an endeavor that we undertake alone. In order to travel the whole distance with Jesus, we need companions for the journey.

Mapping the Way

I never walk an unfamiliar trail or city sidewalk without putting a map in my pocket. Maps help us know where we are going and how to get back home. On the night of his betrayal,

Jesus tells his disciples that he is leaving to prepare a place for them and they know the way to where he will be. Thomas objects, saying that he has no idea where to find Jesus. Could Jesus please be more specific? Jesus answers, I am the true and living Way. (See John 14:1-6.) Thomas wants a map where he can put his finger on the red X that reads, "You are here." Thomas will later want to put that same finger into Jesus' wounded side to gain certainty that Jesus is the Risen One.

Thomas's desire to know the way probably sounds familiar. In times of confusion or disorientation, we often pepper our speech with mapping metaphors. We describe ourselves as "lost at sea" or having "lost our bearings." We say that we "cannot find our way" and "don't know which way to turn." Maps provide a way to orient ourselves.

The history of maps reflects this need for control and prediction. When I hike a trail in the United Kingdom, I always use an Ordnance Survey map. The first Ordnance Survey began in 1791 when the Trigonometrical Survey of the Board of Ordnance was created. The operative word here is *ordnance*, as in munitions and artillery. In the 1790s, England's leaders feared invasion from revolutionary France. Generals and admirals needed detailed, accurate maps to help them position troops and guns. Hence the birth of the Ordnance Survey. Once the threat of French invasion ended, leaders valued the Ordnance Survey maps for another equally important reason. They became indispensable tools for land taxation and determining representation in Parliament.

But maps are powerful tools not only because they help us to predict and plan. Maps also inspire our imaginations.

They allow us to dream of worlds that are not hemmed in or restricted by the realities of our present experience. Children love maps because they let them travel to unknown worlds: The map of Middle Earth in *The Hobbit*, the pirate map in *Treasure Island,* the map of Winnie-the-Pooh's "100 Aker Wood," or the maps on the board games we played as children. Jesus offers this kind of map to Thomas.

Most Bibles contain an appendix of maps. Usually these maps include the boundaries of the Twelve Tribes, the Kingdoms of David and Solomon, Moses' route to the Promised Land, Paul's missionary journeys, or Roman Judea. As a child, I pored over these maps. I would run my finger along the dotted lines that plotted Paul's missionary journeys. I would trace my finger along the walls that encircled Jerusalem. These maps fired my imagination and invited me to go places with God that I never would have dreamed possible.

When I look at a map, I notice all the places that I have not visited. Maps encourage me to dream about places that I want to go and see. In the same way, scripture as a map of God's world lures us to envision unexplored possibilities for ourselves or for our world. The Bible maps out the path to a peaceable kingdom where the lion and the lamb feed together and a small child leads them. (See Isaiah 11:6.) Scripture shows us the way to a world where justice rolls "down like waters, and righteousness like an ever-flowing stream" (Amos 5:24). It describes the dimensions of the New Jerusalem that comes down from heaven and in which God will wipe away every tear and death will be no more. (See Revelation 21:4.)

Scripture as a map of God's path directs my feet toward a more caring, true, and living Way. When I step onto this particular path, I can let go of my need to control, to limit, or to judge others. I no longer crave predictability or certainty in the people and events around me. Instead, I experience a God of grace who invites me to walk imaginatively in others' shoes and to see the world from their perspectives. This map turns my world upside down and changes how I pray.

Sometimes I walk through the aisles of a mall or a grocery store and suddenly realize that I have stepped onto this true and living Way. I have stepped into a thin place of annunciation. And this Way demands a response from me. I look up and see parents struggling with their children, raising their voices and uttering harsh words. I step around a corner and see someone who lives on the edge of poverty carefully looking for the cheapest product on the shelf. I walk into the pharmacy and hear someone talk to the pharmacist about chemotherapy pills. I realize these persons travel a painful, frightening, and lonely path. I walk through the woods and am unexpectedly overwhelmed at how the trees suffer silently as the climate slowly changes.

In each case, the way I am walking becomes a thoroughfare encounter that demands a response from me. These encounters prompt me to pray for those parents and children, for the woman putting chemotherapy pills in her purse, for the unemployed worker who cannot afford the abundance displayed on supermarket shelves, or for policy makers who resist making hard choices about our planet's well-being. These moments of annunciation challenge me to live differently in order to make a difference. They challenge me to walk more intentionally on the way to loving, knowing, and serving God and neighbor. There is no other Way. There is no other map to the thin places where we meet God on the road.

Walking Suggestions

This chapter has explored how walking a path, trail, sidewalk, or road prayerfully and mindfully can cultivate an awareness of other people, their needs, and the ways in which those we meet may be messengers of God who bring insights and invitations to ministry. Here are two walking suggestions for this week based on these themes.

Praying as You Walk

Take a walk this week in which you intentionally go somewhere you will likely encounter people: a shopping mall, a commercial street, a supermarket, or a department store.

Begin your walk by becoming conscious of your body and breathing. If it seems appropriate, use some of the practices suggested in the previous chapters. Then gently shift your awareness to the people and the objects or stores around you. Be curious about them. What catches your attention? What calls to you?

Let the people, objects, or activities you notice become prompts for brief, sentence-like prayers. If you walk past an empty store, you might pray for people who have lost their jobs because a business closed. If you walk past a school, you can pray for the safety of children at school or for those who teach and learn. If it is a school where you know students and teachers, you could pray for them by name.

When you return from your walk, write in a journal about your walk. What moments of annunciation did you experience? Who were the angels you met without knowing it? How did offering a brief prayer for the people and situations you encountered change your experience?

A Discernment Walk

This method differs from the ones above. Rather than using the rhythm of your stride as a mental and spiritual focus, you are invited to let your unconscious mind take over.

Begin with the stretching and breathing exercises outlined in the first Walking Suggestion.

Before you step off, identify a particular issue with which you are struggling. Then forget about it. Do not try to come up with solutions. Do not think about the question or the issue underlying it. Simply relax and let your mind work without any conscious interference. The goal is to think without thinking. If a solution or answer does not come during this walk, try it again on the next walk or the following one. The answer may come days later or at a time other than when you are walking.

Conclude with the stretching exercises, prayers, and journaling outlined in the first Walking Suggestion.

Questions for Further Reflection

1. Pick some of the "thoroughfare" encounters in Luke's Gospel or the book of Acts that I list in this chapter and read them. Look for the common patterns. What do these biblical passages teach you about walking the Way with Jesus? What other thoroughfare encounters in scripture can you recall? How do these stories speak to your own experience?

2. What special road or path do you recall in your life? What memories does it hold for you? In what ways is it a palimpsest or a thin place?

3. Recall any angelic annunciation or thoroughfare encounter you have had. How did the experience affect your spiritual life?

4. Name the companions who walk with you. When have you helped another pilgrim along the Way?

5. What boundary-crossing encounters with strangers have you had? How did these experiences change you?

 ## five

Coming Home

The American naturalist Henry David Thoreau once observed that half of every walk is nothing more than retracing our steps as we go back home. He should know. In his essay "Walking," Thoreau describes how he sauntered almost daily in the fields and pastures around Concord. According to Thoreau, the verb "saunter" derives from medieval pilgrims and crusaders who walked the roads of Europe on their way to the Holy Land—the Saint Terre. Eventually *saint terre* became "saunter." Thoreau later suggests another derivation. Pilgrims and crusaders were *sans terre* or "without land" because they had left home and taken to the road.[1] In either case, Thoreau proposes that to go for a walk is to become a pilgrim, a wayfarer who leaves the safety of home in search of holy ground.

Yet whatever long, winding roads wayfarers travel, their steps usually lead them back to their own doorsteps.

Walking as Pilgrimage

For centuries, faithful Jews journeyed to and from the Jerusalem temple for Israel's three pilgrim festivals: Passover, Tabernacles, and Weeks or Dedication. (Read Exodus 23:14-16.) Luke's Gospel tells how Jesus and his family went to Jerusalem for the Passover and then returned to Nazareth. (See Luke 2:41-51.) John's Gospel describes Jesus as going to Jerusalem for all three pilgrim festivals and then returning to Galilee. (See John 2:13-22; 7:1-11; 10:22-23.)

Early Christians continued this tradition of pilgrimage. They traveled to sacred sites associated with Jesus, the early apostles, or martyrs and saints. Most pilgrims returned home with a deepened faith and exotic stories to tell their friends and neighbors. As early as 333 CE, an anonymous pilgrim from Bordeaux traveled to Palestine and returned home to write a detailed travelogue. Between 381 and 384 CE, a nun named Egeria traveled to the Holy Land from her convent somewhere on the Atlantic coast of Spain or Gaul. She later wrote an account of her pilgrimage, which remains a basic resource for understanding early Christian worship in Jerusalem.

Some pilgrims left home with no intention of returning. Among Celtic Christians, some monks embraced "white martyrdom" and became permanent wanderers. Theirs were not martyrdoms of blood but of walking forever in Ireland's white mist and fog. Most pilgrims, however, embraced a rhythm of leaving and returning home—a rhythm not unlike the stance-and-swing cadence of our feet.

The motives of these early Christian pilgrims are strikingly similar to those of contemporary wayfarers and walkers. Both seek to go beyond their normal routines. By disrupting everyday patterns, they hope to encounter something new that fills them with awe or wonder. The pilgrim seeks a shrine flooded with the light of a thousand votive candles; the walker may seek a bird's nest cradling three small blue-green eggs. Both seek wholeness or well-being. They both sense a loss of vitality in their everyday lives that they may find again by taking to their feet.

These similarities explain why the numbers of people going on pilgrimages have exploded at virtually the same time that more people walk for health, leisure, or transportation. The Way of Saint James in Spain, for example, increased from around 2,500 pilgrims in 1985–86 to nearly 238,000 in 2014.

Curiously, church pews have emptied out across Europe and North America during these same years. As people have turned away from traditional religious institutions and beliefs, they have sought the sacred by walking ancient pilgrimage routes, the Appalachian Trail, or even the treadmill at the local gym. Egeria's book on her pilgrimage to Jerusalem has been replaced by Cheryl Strayed's *Wild: From Lost to Found on the Pacific Crest Trail*. Both relate tales of personal transformation triggered by walking as a form of pilgrimage. One is ancient and deeply Christian; the other, secular and contemporary. The desire to take to our feet signifies a genuine search for spiritual connection in a world where many people have abandoned organized religion yet still yearn for the sacred. This phenomenon raises an important question: What would happen if churches responded to this yearning by inviting people to explore walking as a Christian practice?

Transforming the Landscape of the Heart

If Thoreau's portrayal of every walker as a pilgrim is accurate, no matter how brief the journey, then, when we go for a walk, we are seeking a place in the physical landscape that corresponds to a place in the soul's inner landscape. We journey outward, hoping that our steps will take us on an inward, spiritual voyage.

Herman Melville, one of Thoreau's contemporaries, experienced this outward/inward journey. Disappointed by public reception to what he considered his greatest work, *Moby Dick*, Melville entered a period of personal and professional crisis. In the midst of this crisis, he traveled to the Holy Land. Later he abandoned writing novels and turned instead to poetry. His most famous long poem is *Clarel: A Poem and Pilgrimage in the Holy Land*, one of the longest poems in American literature, stretching to more than eighteen thousand lines.

Clarel, the poem's main character, is a young theology student in the midst of a crisis of faith. He sets out on a pilgrimage to the Holy Land, which parallels the trip that Melville himself took. Clarel's pilgrimage ultimately is less a search for shrines and churches than a journey through the inner landscape of his soul as he wrestles with what he really believes. He seeks places in the rugged landscape of the Holy Land that correspond to the ragged places of his inner, spiritual landscape.

A short story by French author Marguerite Yourcenar retells a Chinese fable in which the master painter Wang-Fo paints such beautiful pictures that they cast a harsh shadow over reality itself. Since the emperor finds such prophetic beauty a threat to his power, he imprisons the painter and plans to kill him. Wang-Fo saves his life by using the only tools at his disposal. He paints a beautiful seascape. He even paints himself into his picture, sitting in a boat. Finally, merging himself with the figure of himself that he has painted, Wang-Fo escapes by sailing away into his own landscape.

Wang-Fo escapes by finding a correspondence between something within himself and something in his landscape. Clarel travels to the Holy Land searching for some experience in the physical world around him that will resolve his inner anguish. To discover such moments of correspondence between our outer and inner landscapes is to enter into a freeing, sacred space. The spiritual practice of walking invites us to discover such moments of correspondence in the cadence of our legs.

We do not need to hike the Pacific Crest Trail or go to Jerusalem to be on a pilgrimage, however. Places of pilgrimage are as close as our doorstep. Every time we go for a walk, we go on a mini-pilgrimage. We do not simply walk to the supermarket for milk, go to the gym to use the treadmill, or stroll through the neighborhood park. Wherever our feet carry us can become a pilgrimage into the sacred.

With the rise of Muslim kingdoms in the eastern Mediterranean, Christian pilgrimages to the Holy Land became more difficult, dangerous, and infrequent. But medieval Christians did not stop being pilgrims. They found other ways to go on pilgrimage that were closer to home.

One alternative was a cloister. A cloister is a covered walk or arcade that links various parts of a monastery or cathedral complex. Builders typically placed one cloister arcade into the wall of a cathedral or church. The other three sides connected the monastery's scriptorium, kitchen, chapter house, dormitories, or infirmary to the church and each other. Cloisters served a practical purpose. They linked different buildings under the cover of one roof. They also had a religious and spiritual purpose. Processions and other ceremonies took place along these arcaded walkways. Cloisters also created a sheltered place where people could walk, converse, or think. As persons walked the cloister's arcades, they could go on a mini-pilgrimage. The cloister's arcades suggest that any path can become a spiritual path.

A garden was usually at the center of a cloister. This garden, sometimes called a garth, might have a single tree growing in the middle. It symbolized the tree of life that God planted at the center of the Garden of Eden. Other garths had a water fountain, which symbolized the fountain in the book of Revelation, flowing from beneath God's throne and giving life to the tree whose leaves are for the healing of the nations. (See Revelation 22:2.) Walking the cloister's arcades, believers could discover new insights into the soul's journey to God.

Enclosed shopping malls offer modern cloisters. They too contain trees and fountains. People come to walk and talk in their broad hallways. Unfortunately, these modern "cloisters" suggest a very different correspondence between inner and outer landscapes. They seduce us into believing we can fill the empty places of our hearts with consumption of goods.

My congregation has a modern adaptation of the cloister. Alongside the sanctuary building lies a garden planted with flowering shrubs and perennials. An education wing wraps around this small garden. Its hallways look out onto the garden through a series of glass panels and columns meant to resemble a cloister. In pleasant weather, workers from downtown offices walk to our cloistered garden to relax, talk, and eat their lunches. When I look out and see them, I sometimes think about those medieval cloisters. Our visitors are a far cry from medieval monks and nuns. But they share the same yearning for a transformative correspondence between their inner and outer landscapes. My church's lunch-hour visitors seek a place that frees them from the confines of their daily existence. They walk to our garden to discover a physical space where they may find wholeness and inner peace.

Coming Home

Pilgrimages begin for many reasons, but they always end at the same place: home. People often describe the Christian life as a journey or a pilgrimage. We are a pilgrim people. We are marching to Zion. We are pilgrims and exiles on earth. (See Hebrews 11:13.) *Pilgrimage* and *journey* may be two of the most frequent words we use to describe the Christian life.

But what about images of home and homecoming? The Bible does not lack for stories of home and homecoming.

Ruth and Naomi return to Naomi's home village when they find themselves widowed in Moab. Judean exiles return home to Jerusalem after seventy years by the waters of Babylon. Having been warned in a dream not to return to King Herod, the magi return to their home country by another road. After Herod's death, the holy family returns home to Nazareth. The prodigal returns home to the waiting father. On the night of his betrayal and arrest, Jesus tells his disciples that he is going home to his Father and will prepare a place for them because "in my Father's house there are many dwelling places" (John 14:2). Home and homecoming are neglected images in Christian spirituality despite the Bible's many references to them.

Why? Perhaps the image of home connotes work rather than joy, domination rather than freedom. For some people, home is a place of danger and threat, of domestic violence and abuse. Home is also where injuries and accidents can happen. People fall down the stairs. They slip on the rug and break their hip. Home can evoke images of loneliness. Parents suffer from empty-nest syndrome. A widow or widower returns home to an empty house that no longer feels like home. Children learn that growing up means leaving home. To return home means you have failed to establish yourself as an independent adult.

Yet home also holds out an image of hope and promise. We come home for Christmas. We go home to God at the end of our lives. Home can represent an emotional and spiritual shelter amid the storms of life. In his poem "The Death of the Hired Man," Robert Frost writes, "Home is the place where, when you have to go there, they have to take you in."

Many of us feel a tension between the urge to be on the road and the yearning to go home. On the one hand, home can feel safe, wrapped in a cocoon of security. On the other hand, traveling the open road leaves us free to experiment and enjoy the excitement of whatever might happen next.

But I believe another choice exists. To be a pilgrim or a walker combines the best qualities of both wanderers and homebodies. Pilgrims recognize that the path leading away from home is the same path that brings us back. Walkers can thus enjoy the surprises of the journey and of the homecoming. This openness to surprise or awe defines hope. When we think nothing can change enough to surprise us, we have lost all hope.

The labyrinth, like the cloister, represents another medieval alternative to long-distance pilgrimages. Labyrinths reveal how the journey and the homecoming are two aspects of one experience. When the routes to Jerusalem became too dangerous to travel, churches inscribed large spiraling pathways—labyrinths—into their floors to create a virtual pilgrimage. These circuits led to a center, which represented the New Jerusalem, heaven, or perhaps the heart of God. Just like Thoreau's journeys there and back again, the path to the center is the same path that leads back out. The labyrinth thus suggests several truths about walking as a spiritual practice.

First, we find our way to the center after we have traveled the whole circle. There are no shortcuts to wisdom, insight, or spiritual wholeness. The long way leads to the goal we prize the most.

Second, we do not find our deepest truths until we can draw into our awareness the whole circumference of our experiences. We must walk all the circuits of the labyrinth, drawing them into ourselves, before we reach the center. In the same way, we find our true home with God by inclusion, not exclusion. We discover God's grace when we accept the whole of who we are, not when we deny or suppress the wounded parts of ourselves that we feel too ashamed to share with God, who longs to heal us. We experience God's grace when we include outsiders who have been excluded and call them our companions.

Third, the labyrinth's cross-shaped design holds the overall pattern together. Ultimately, we do not so much hold on to the cross as the cross holds on to us. It structures who we are. The cross directs our feet along the path God calls us to walk.

Fourth, the twists and turns of the labyrinth's circuits mean that we frequently turn our backs on the final destination—the labyrinth's center—before reaching it. Likewise, we sometimes have to turn our backs on our most important goals to order to reach them.

Fifth, we walk the same twists and turns going out of the labyrinth as we walked on our journey to its center. In the same way, life does not necessarily become less complicated or difficult after we give ourselves to Christ. However, we now know the One who walks with us.

Sixth, as we walk the labyrinth, we seem immediately to approach the center. Then suddenly the path turns, and we are unexpectedly walking the outermost circuit. Conversely, we can be walking on the outer circuits and then, just a few steps later, we find ourselves entering the center. In our everyday lives, we often cannot tell how close or distant we are from achieving our goals. We may actually be close, but we feel like we will never reach them. Walking the labyrinth provides a lesson in perseverance and not losing hope. Walking as a spiritual practice helps us live with intentionality, hope, and wonder as faithful disciples of Jesus Christ.

Pilgrims and Pedestrians, Peons and Pawns

In a world addicted to speed, most people are passengers rather than pedestrians. Rather than have wings and wheels, those who walk have only their own two feet beneath them. When we walk, we no longer possess the power and privilege of speed. Walking identifies us with the poor and the poor in Spirit, the orphan and the widow, the marginal and the invisible ones.

As far back as humans can remember, walking or sitting has separated the wealthy and powerful from everyone else. The rich and powerful sat. They sat atop a horse or in a horse-drawn chariot. They sat in a litter carried on the shoulders of slaves. Everyone else walked. Because the common person walked, one of the easiest ways to distinguish yourself as wealthy and important came in exercising the privilege of "taking a load off your feet."

This distinction still exists in our contemporary world. The rich and powerful move in a world of speed and convenience. The more money, the more technological prostheses.

Technologies buy speed, comfort, and convenience—our modern equivalents of the ancient world's horse-drawn and slave-borne litters. Like horses and slaves, speed and comfort signify status and access to power. It is not by accident that we describe the superelite as "the jet set."

The men and women of the Bible did not fall into the "jet-set" elite. They were people who walked under the power of their own two feet. Moses' band of refugees and slaves walk through the parted waters. But Yahweh clogs the wheels of Pharaoh's chariots. (See Exodus 14:25, 29.) The author of Exodus makes a point of mentioning Pharaoh's horses and chariots twelve times in twelve verses when describing how Israel escaped from Egypt. (Read Exodus 14:17-28.) Our scriptures were written by, to, and for people who walked—the poor, the marginal, the invisible.

In Latin, the root *ped* means "foot." A *pedes* was a soldier who went on foot, as opposed to the wealthy equestrian class of knights who could afford a war horse and had experience riding. A foot soldier was vulnerable and expendable. The Hebrew word for soldiers is *raglim*, from the root *rgl* or "foot." Whereas kings and nobles fought from a chariot or on horseback, the lowly combat soldier advanced into battle by foot. Throughout most of human history, armies fought on their feet. They marched into battle. In our contemporary world, wheels and wings have changed even this reality. The modern army has traded boots for wheels. Troops no longer march into battle. They pile into an armored personnel carrier and are driven into combat. The words "let's roll" have replaced "forward march."

Ped is also the root for "peon." By the middle ages, the Latin word for a foot soldier had evolved into the word describing a serf or laborer: A *pedonem*. To be a peon, a "foot," is to be an insignificant worker at the mercy of those with power and status. The Bible also uses the term *foot* as a metaphor for slavery. Deuteronomy 11:10 contrasts Israelite freedom to the oppression of Egyptian slaves who must use their feet to power the water pumps that irrigate Pharaoh's fields. When we speak of a farm or field "hand" we mean precisely what both Deuteronomy and medieval kings meant when they called someone a peon or a "foot"—someone of low status, an undocumented worker, someone hired cheaply to do menial labor. Peons pick our tomatoes, clean our houses, or mow our lawns. The higher our social or economic status, the more power and privilege we enjoy, both of which allow us to hire a "hand" or a "foot" to do our bidding.

The Latin root *ped* likewise underlies the name for the humblest, least powerful piece on a chessboard: the pawn. It moves slowly across the board one square at a time. Rooks, knights, and bishops can leap across the board, but a pawn has limited mobility. Pawns are plentiful and can be sacrificed for the sake of more valuable pieces. In our everyday speech, to call people "pawns" is to label them as weak, powerless, and easily controlled by others.

Our word *pedestrian* also derives from the Latin *ped*. It originally meant "plain, not in verse": *pedestris*. Pedestrian writing plods along in a flat-footed way. It does not soar and sing like poetry. The very word *pedestrian* carries a slight hint of suspicion. We often view those who walk as people who are too impoverished to own a car or pay for insurance. They are the down-and-out whose licenses have been revoked for drunk driving, drug abuse, or other crimes. If we remember that Jesus was a pedestrian, what does this say about our attitudes toward those who are compelled to walk in a society that moves on wheels and wings?

Walking, that most fundamental of human acts, automatically makes us pedestrians, peons, pawns in someone else's game. Engraved in our language is the notion that those who walk are less important than those who sit or ride. In Asia, a wandering monk performs a sacred function, but we in our culture label such wanderers as vagrants and arrest them for loitering.

Those who sit and ride receive no challenge to offer hospitality. They are not confronted with thoroughfare encounters or unexpected annunciations. High off the ground as they ride along, they look down on pedestrians. They never have to make eye contact with strangers. No wonder we label proud or haughty people as being "on their high horse"!

Walking as a spiritual practice repeatedly introduces us to a God who moves at the speed of a footstep and embraces the peon, the pawn, and the pedestrian. This God moves at a pedestrian pace and looks with mercy on the poor and the marginalized.

Homemaking in God's Reign

When I am a pedestrian, I voluntarily displace myself from my advantages of speed and privilege and consequently identify with the millions of involuntarily displaced people across the globe: refugees of war, famine, or ecological catastrophe, and the rural exodus that has ballooned cities into teeming metropolises awash in poverty and hunger. Walking ought to increase my solidarity with the marginalized and impoverished who have no choice but to walk. If I go for a walk and return home without a deeper commitment to homemaking for all God's people, then I may have been a tourist on a trip but not a pilgrim on the Way of Jesus.

My congregation participates in the annual community CROP Walk for Hunger. We can easily reduce this event to a discrete activity on the church's program calendar or to celebrate the generosity of our members and how much money they raise. The participants' experience of the annual CROP Walk would be more transforming if we helped one another to see more clearly the correspondence between our walking and the path that refugees and migrants must walk each day.

When citizens feel disenfranchised and alienated from the political system, they walk or march to express their anger and frustration. Many of my congregants participate in various protest marches. Marching for a cause bears public testimony to God's call to homemaking and good housekeeping.

A great deal of modern history bears the imprint of protesters' feet. Protesters marched from Selma to Montgomery to challenge an American system of racial segregation and oppression. Beginning in 1977, mothers of "the disappeared" marched weekly around the Plaza de Mayo in Buenos Aires, demanding to know who was responsible for their children's deaths and where authorities had disposed of their bodies.

Their walks played a crucial role in ending the military junta that ruled Argentina. Between 1986 and 1991, people in the Baltic Republics of Estonia, Latvia, and Lithuania marched in the streets and sang national songs as a protest against Soviet domination. History is made on the soles of our feet.

Perhaps this explains why the leaders of the two most transformative social movements of the twentieth century both use the metaphor of walking to describe their work. Nelson Mandela's *Long Walk to Freedom* tells the story of the struggle to end apartheid in South Africa. Martin Luther King Jr. titled the story of the Montgomery bus boycott *Stride toward Freedom*. Both titles employ walking metaphors to describe the struggle for more just and equitable societies. The analogy to walking suggests that we cannot hurry genuine social transformation. Anything worth accomplishing cannot be rushed. Kingdom work requires patience and a long view because our three-mile-per-hour God works slowly and quietly in human history.

Stepping Out in the Public Square

Stepping out in the public square as a form of Christian witness can take many forms: protest marches, walks for hunger. These activities do not exhaust the list of possibilities, however.

Early in 2014, Jennifer Howard, a member of Trinity Episcopal Church in Marshall, Texas, approached her rector with a new idea.[2] She proposed that Trinity Church sponsor a "prayer walk" in Marshall. On the day of Trinity Church's Prayer Walk, about one hundred and twenty people gathered in Trinity's sanctuary for an opening prayer service. They then walked through downtown Marshall lifting every part of the community in prayer. After the walk, everyone joined in a cookout as a way for Trinity's members to get to know some of the community residents who participated in the walk.

When Jennifer shared her idea for a Prayer Walk with her rector, she was surprised to discover that prayer walks are nothing new. In fact, her rector explained that even before the Norman Conquest, English parish churches sponsored an annual prayer walk, which they called "beating the bounds." In an age when maps were a rarity, knowing the boundaries of territory was critically important. So once a year everyone in the parish would walk its boundaries. They would stop and inspect boundary markers as well as pray for fields, crops, homes, and livestock along the way. Some English parishes still observe an annual Beating of the Bounds. Once, in an English grocery store, I saw a poster about a local official who was raising funds for charities in a novel way. He planned to walk around the bounds of his local parish, and he asked sponsors to donate to one of these charities for every mile that he walked.

Other English parishes have capitalized on people's interest in walking. While walking Hadrian's Path Trail in northern England, I took a side trail that is part of St. Oswald's Way. A local Anglican priest charted out a walking trail that crosses Northumberland from Lindisfarne, or The Holy Island, in the north, to Heavensfield in the south. The ninety-seven-mile route takes walkers past sites associated with the Celtic Christian bishop Saint Oswald, who was instrumental in Christianizing England. I have sometimes thought that churches in a particular geographic region might come together to create and publicize similar walking trails for people who desire a mini-pilgrimage to sites of spiritual or historical significance in their area.

Followers of Jesus have a long history of pilgrimage. Like the circuits of a labyrinth, the Christian journey contains twists and turns. Yet we can trust that the path and the goal are one, and, even when we wander from the path, God's strong hands guide us back home. For the journey, we need sturdy shoes on our feet, not wheels and wings. "As shoes for your feet put on whatever will make you ready to proclaim the gospel of peace" (Eph. 6:15). We walk with a God who loves the peon and the pawn, the marginal and the vulnerable. The God who guides our feet in the way of peace (Luke 1:79) has told us what is good and what the Lord requires of us: "to do justice, and to love kindness, and to walk humbly with your God" (Mic. 6:8).

Thomas A. Dorsey's hymn "Precious Lord, Take My Hand" ends with a prayer that God in Christ, his precious Lord, will lead him home. This prayer lies at the heart of walking as a spiritual discipline. As followers of the Way, we pray that God will take our hands, guide our feet, and lead us home.

Walking Suggestions

In this chapter we have examined the themes of pilgrims and pilgrimage. Few of us have opportunities to travel to faraway shrines and pilgrimage centers. Yet all of us can experience pilgrimage. The first exercise invites you to find a labyrinth or Stations of the Cross to walk as a mini-pilgrimage. Our journeys away from home on pilgrimage usually bring us back home as changed people. The second exercise explores the experience of homecoming after a walk.

Go on a Mini-Pilgrimage

Find a park, retreat center, or church near you that has a labyrinth and walk it. If none is located near you, most Roman Catholic congregations or retreat centers have either indoor or outdoor Stations of the Cross. Churches, retreat centers, or other organizations will usually provide interpretive materials and prayer resources when walking their labyrinth or Stations of the Cross.

After you have completed your walk, take time to make some notes in your journal about your experience of walking the labyrinth or Stations of the Cross.

Coming Home

On a street map, mark the location of your home or office. Depending on where you work or live, this exercise may require two maps.

Draw a circle that encompasses everything within a fifteen-minute walk of your home or office. Within this circle, identify specific places to which you usually drive. List these places on a separate sheet of paper. Then prioritize the places to which you could walk if you chose to do so, with your first choice being "# 1."

Make a commitment this week to walk to the store, shop, home, or office that you listed as your number-one priority.

Even if the weather is less than ideal or you feel pressed for time, keep with this commitment to walk rather than drive.

Be particularly attentive to your experiences of returning home as well as of getting to know your immediate neighborhood better. Reflect on how walking around your home each day changed your week, your use of time. What was the experience of returning to your own home each day like? In what ways did you return home a slightly different person? You will want to record these observations in your walking journal.

Questions for Further Reflection

1. When have you gone on a pilgrimage to a place that is sacred to you? This could include a visit to a religious shrine, but it could also include visiting a presidential home or library; the home of a famous author, poet, artist, or musician whom you admire. It could be the site of a battle or historical event significant to you. For some, the journey back to a family home or church is a pilgrimage. What was your pilgrimage like? What distinction would you draw between being a "pilgrim" and being a "tourist"?

2. The words *pilgrim* and *pilgrimage* suggest a twofold movement of going out and coming home. How do you respond to the idea that a pilgrim holds in tension the wanderer's desire to keep moving and the homebody's desire to stay safe? Would you describe yourself more as a wanderer, a homebody, or a pilgrim?

3. When you hear the word *home*, what feelings or images come to mind? Are they mostly positive, negative, or a mixture of both? How do these feelings and images influence your response to the biblical concept of home and homecoming?

4. Recall a time when you encountered something in the physical landscape that corresponded to—or spoke to—a particular place in the landscape of your heart or soul. How did God touch your life through this experience?

5. When you see people walking along a street or highway, what assumptions do you make about them? What prejudices do you have about people who seem to have no car? How does this chapter's perspective on "pedestrians" shape or reshape your assumptions or prejudices?

six

Guide My Feet

Humans are travelers. We define ourselves physically, psychologically, and spiritually by movement. Our feet carry us through space and time. They take us to places in nature. They carry us to places of the heart. As disciples of Jesus Christ, we walk between time and eternity. We identify who we are by how we move.

In the 1970s, researchers at Wesleyan University asked six students to participate in an experiment. All six students knew one another and were roughly the same size. Researchers asked them to put on dark clothing. They then wrapped reflective tape around each student's ankles, knees, elbows, wrists, hips, and shoulders. The researchers next asked the students to walk across a dimly lit room as they filmed them. Researchers later adjusted the lighting on the film so only the bright color of the reflective tape was visible. A few months later, researchers invited the same six students to watch the film. The students could not distinguish faces or other personal features. They could only see glowing, blurry dots moving across a dark screen. The researchers asked the students to identify themselves and one another based solely on the movements of the glowing dots as they bounced and bobbed across the screen. Their identifications were surprisingly accurate.[1]

Like these students, most people can recognize themselves and their close acquaintances simply by their gait and stride. Each of us has a slightly different way of walking. Eadweard Muybridge, who took photographs of trotting horses, also published sequences of humans walking or leapfrogging over one another. Like the Wesleyan University researchers, Muybridge discovered that no two people walk in precisely the same way. We speed up and slow down at different points in our stride. We swing our arms in highly individualized ways. Some people keep their knees straight and stiff as they walk; others flex their knees. Our gaits are as unique as our fingerprints. Our identities begin at the tips of our toes.

When we walk with others, we notice these individual differences. Starting off in a group, we sometimes cannot quite find a shared rhythm. Eventually we ease into some semblance of a shared pace. "Will two people walk together unless they have agreed to do so?" (3:3, CEB) asks the prophet Amos. When we walk, each of us brings his or her own unique stride. Yet we also have to agree on a shared rhythm.

Is learning to walk with God any different? Our human gait does not automatically fall into sync with God's stride. With time, discipline, and prayer we eventually attune our stride to God's rhythm. This attunement requires that we shift our attention from ourselves and instead pay attention to the direction of God's energy.

The Ten Commandments prohibit Israel from making graven images. Prophets like Isaiah repeatedly condemn the sin of idolatry. According to Isaiah, idols are static. They do not move. On the other hand, the very essence of Israel's God is movement. Moses will only glimpse God in motion as God walks past the cleft in the rock that shelters Moses. You cannot make a static image of a God who is constantly in motion.

Every Footprint Tells a Story

Should it surprise us then that people recognize the One who becomes the human face of God by the movement of his feet? Pilgrims visiting Jerusalem since the time of the Bordeaux pilgrim and Egeria have visited a small shrine on the Mount of Olives. Inside the eight-sided Chapel of the Ascension is a stone frame set into the floor. This frame contains what pilgrims venerate as Jesus' right footprint, which he left behind as he ascended to heaven. This footprint signifies not just Jesus' ascension from this world. It also exemplifies every footprint he ever made on the dusty roads of Galilee. It is the token of the bloody footprints he left on his way to the cross. The whole gospel resides in this single footprint.

Each person's footprints are as unique as his or her stride or gait. Each has its own story to tell. The iconic photograph of Neil Armstrong's left footprint pressed into the moon's dusty surface, for example, tells a story of science and courage reaching back into history and projecting into the future. Like Paleolithic handprints on cave walls, footprints are a sign language of a uniquely human presence that we all understand.

Who has not felt a sense of curiosity about a series of unknown footprints in freshly fallen snow? Who has not wondered about the footprints we see on a sandy beach? Footprints have the power to draw us in. Their shape and spacing cradle within them an element of mystery. When we walk beside these silent reminders of someone else's presence, we unconsciously match our gait to theirs. We know vaguely that, if only momentarily, we have stepped into someone else's story.

"For we walk by faith, not by sight," Paul writes to the Corinthians (2 Cor. 5:7). It certainly requires a leap of faith to see the outline of Jesus' right foot in a misshapen rock on the Mount of Olives. At the same time, footprints in the snow or sand invite us to look beyond sight alone and to step, if only briefly, into the mystery of their unseen makers. They invite us to walk by faith, not by sight.

Footprints in sand, mud, or snow are ephemeral phenomena. They do not last forever. Falling snow can obliterate them. The tide can wash them away. Their duration is part of the cycle of nature itself. "All people are grass, their constancy is like the flower of the field," proclaims the prophet Isaiah. Footprints remind us how the things of this world are always passing away. "But the word of our God will stand forever" (Isa. 40:6, 8).

The spiritual practice of walking reminds us that so much of what we see and experience is transitory and passing. We are therefore to let what endures be the focus of our lives. First Peter quotes Isaiah's words comparing God's eternal word to the ephemeral nature of human life. Then he says to his readers, "Now that you have purified your souls by your obedience to the truth so that you have genuine mutual love, love one another deeply from the heart" (1:22). Walking by faith, not sight, often means letting God's truth and compassion be the focus of our lives.

Footprints on the Beach

In May 2013, along the Norfolk coast of England, scientists made a crucial discovery in British archaeology. Rough seas had eroded a sandy beach near the town of Happisburgh. At low tide, a series of elongated hollows became visible along the beach—the earliest known human footprints outside Africa. They may be eight hundred thousand years old.[2]

Rain and the rising tide soon erased the footprints, but not before scientists had videotaped and photographed them. Later analysis showed them to be the footprints of as many as five people. The adult male was perhaps five feet, nine inches tall and weighed approximately one hundred and ten pounds. The shortest was about three feet in height. The other three ranged in size and age; one of them may have been an adult female. Their footprints provide a glimpse of what was perhaps a small family group moving across an ancient landscape.

On the opposite side of England, at Formby Point near Liverpool, scientists have discovered the footprints left by another small group of ancestors on a sandy beach. These footprints are not nearly so old as the ones at Happisburgh. They were made only five to seven thousand years ago.[3]

The man who made the prints at Formby Point was six foot three. The woman stood about a foot shorter. Based on the distance between strides, the man was in a hurry. The woman moved more slowly. Smaller footprints suggest children romping in the sand as they walked along the beach, perhaps to gather shellfish.

The footprints at Happisburgh and Formby Point tell the story of specific people and their journeys. We can make educated guesses about their height, their gait, their gender, and even their speed. Their footprints so resemble our own that they seem familiar. Yet they are mysterious because we know so little about the men, women, and children who made them. *Who were they? Why was the man in such a hurry? Where did they come from? Where were they going?*

When I paused at Formby Point and gazed at the waves rolling toward the shore, I wondered if these ancient travelers also paused from their journey at this same spot. Did they too see the Welsh mountains to the south? Were their feet as tired as mine? How many miles would they have to travel before reaching their destination? Separated by several millennia, their lives and mine mingled mysteriously on this beach, if only for the briefest of moments. All of us are pilgrims on a journey to places known and unknown.

Sometimes, when I walk an ancient pilgrim way, I pause at the top of a hill and look into the distance. I wonder if my eyes are seeing what those earlier travelers saw as they passed this same spot. In that moment, I feel a strange kinship with them. In seeing now what they once saw, I become one with them if only in my imagination. Separated by time and space, we are companions on a shared human journey, our footprints imprinted on the same fragile planet we both call home.

At such moments, I do not feel so alone. I am surrounded by a community of others who have made this same human journey. The church calls this sense of shared community across time and space the "communion of saints" and celebrates it on All Saints Day. "Therefore, since we are surrounded by so great a cloud of witnesses, let us also lay aside every weight and the sin that clings so closely, and let us run with perseverance the race that is set before us, looking to Jesus the pioneer and perfecter of our faith" (Heb. 12:1-2).

This time-and-space-bending relationship with our ancient forebears is not so different from the relationship we have with Christians in other parts of the world (or even within our own congregations) whose behavior or beliefs occasionally seem so alien to us. We share a common Christian journey and a shared humanity. We look out on the same world and are members of one communion of saints. Yet each of us has a unique gait. We all belong to God whose grace goes before us and prepares the way for us. Theologians call it prevenient grace.

The scientist in charge of studying the Happisburgh footprints told the BBC News correspondent that the significance of these footprints rested on the knowledge that once researchers realized that modern humans arrived so early in Britain's history, they can look with fresh eyes at the ground beneath their feet. If they keep looking and know what to look for, they will find more evidence of modern humans' presence.

And what about those other feet? The ones that trod the stony trackways of Egypt, those who left their footprints in the mud of the Sea of Reeds and who marched around the city of Jericho until its walls came tumbling down? What about the feet that walked from Galilee to Jerusalem only to be nailed to a cross? Or the disciples whose feet Jesus washed in an upper room on the night he was betrayed? What about the Bordeaux Pilgrim and Egeria who left their footprints on long-forgotten roads to Jerusalem? Now that we know what the traces of God's presence look like, do we have fresh eyes to discover more evidence of God at work in us and in our world?

Walking as Knowing

When I look at those footprints on the beaches at Happisburgh and Formby Point, I realize that none of them moves in an absolutely straight line. They all weave and wander to one side or the other. When you look at a line of footprints, the first thing you notice is that they almost always curve from one side to the other.

Sometimes I draw a line with a ruler. At other times, I draw a freehand line. The freehand line is seldom perfectly straight.

But, like a sidewalk, a line I make with a ruler is straight as an arrow. When I draw a line freehand, I keep my eye on where the pencil is going and make adjustments for the friction on the surface of the paper as I move my hand. This is probably why no footpath is precisely straight. Walkers have to pay continuous attention to their path. They fine-tune their feet as their journey unfolds. The moving itself brings knowing. Like dancing, walking is thinking in movement.

In John's Gospel, two of the Baptizer's disciples come to Jesus, wanting to know more. Jesus says to them, "Come and see" (1:39). When Nathanael asks Philip if anything good can come from Nazareth, Philip does not reason with him, provide him information, or unfold a logical rationale. He simply says, "Come and see" (1:46).

None of Jesus' disciples walks a straight line. They weave and wander. Each has a unique gait and stride. In the end, according to the Synoptic Gospel writers, they walk away and leave him alone on the cross. Few paths are precisely straight or like anyone else's because the path of discipleship is not a sidewalk engineered with a ruler. Disciples of Jesus Christ learn to pay attention to the path as the journey unfolds. Their movement is never something separate from their knowing. It is, in fact, a deepest kind of knowing. As followers of Jesus Christ, we do not get all our ideas about God in their correct order and then follow Jesus. When we walk as a spiritual practice, we know the path of discipleship only as we walk it.

Walking Suggestion

This walking suggestion invites you to reflect on how you can introduce new opportunities for walking as a spiritual practice into your congregation or strengthen existing opportunities for walking as a spiritual practice. As an individual or working with others, make a list of all the events or ministries of your congregation in which walking plays a role: Prayer Walks, CROP Walks, Stations of the Cross, labyrinths, worship processionals, and so forth. Then write them in the appropriate box, using as an example the chart "Your Congregation's Ministry of Walking" on page 126.

Look at the pattern of ministries in your faith community that incorporate walking. Who participates? Who is missing? What resources do they use? What times of the year are overscheduled? underscheduled? How is your congregation helping people draw closer to God through ministries of walking?

Brainstorm the ways people gather to walk in your congregation or community. Possibilities might include the group of older members who regularly walk at the mall or friends who use the treadmills at the gym together. Who might be interested in walking together for health and adding a Bible study component to their exercise?

Look at your worship service. What can be done to help worshipers develop a Christian understanding of how they move their feet in worship?

Now, using the same chart and a different colored marker, add some of your ideas to the chart.

With such a chart, you and other leaders can begin to construct a systemic picture of where various walking ministries are happening, who is now involved or could potentially be involved, and what next steps might be discerned for a ministry of walking in your congregation.

Questions for Further Reflection

1. Who can you recognize from a distance simply by the way they walk?

2. What makes your walk unique? How does knowledge of your distinctive gait alter your view of walking?

3. Describe a time when you walked with others and became aware of the awkwardness of finding a shared rhythm. What resolved the group's awkwardness of trying to walk together? What could you learn from this experience about how we can walk with Christ as diverse congregations?

4. When have you felt close to others who may have walked the same street or trail long ago simply because you all saw the same landscape? What does this experience or image have to say about our solidarity as Christian community?

5. Looking back at the topics and activities you have experienced since opening this book, how will you continue to adapt the many different ways you take to your feet daily so these moments contribute to your spiritual formation as a disciple of Jesus Christ?

Your Congregation's Ministry of Walking

Months of the Year	Event	Who Participates (describe the target audience—age, gender, level of activity in congregation)	Group or Individual Responsible	Resources Used
January				
February				
March				
April				
May				
June				
July				
August				
September				
October				
November				
December				

NOTES

Two   Prime Mover

1. John Keats, *Letters of John Keats to His Family and Friends,* ed. Sidney Colvin (London: Macmillan and Co., 1891), 276–77.

Five   Coming Home

1. Henry David Thoreau, "Walking," *Collected Essays and Poems* (NY: Penguin/Putnam, 2001), 225–26.

2. Magdalena Altnau, M. 2015. "Prayer Walk Blesses City," *The Royal Cross* (Winter 2015): 15-17.

Six   Guide My Feet

1. James E. Cutting, and Lynn T. Kozlowski, "Recognizing friends by their walk: Gait perception without familiarity cues," *Bulletin of the Psychonomic Society*, vol. 9 (5): 353–56.

2. Kate Wong, "Human Footprints Discovered on England's Coast Are Oldest Outside Africa." *Scientific American*, February 7, 2014. http://blogs.scientificamerican.com/observations/2014/02/07/human-footprints-discovered-on-englands-coast-are-oldest-outside-africa/ (retrieved 3/25/15) and Pallab Ghosh, "Earliest footprints outside Africa discovered in Norfolk." BBC News/Science & Environment. http://www.bbc.com/news/science-environment-26025763 (retrieved 3/25/15).

3. Barry Cunliffe, *Britain Begins* (Oxford: Oxford University Press, 2013), 126–27.

CPSIA information can be obtained
at www.ICGtesting.com
Printed in the USA
LVOW04s0456160416

483725LV00004B/4/P